Win!

Win!

Compelling Conversations with 20 Successful South Africans

Jeremy Maggs

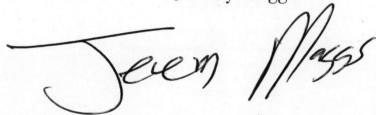

JACANA

First published by Jacana Media (Pty) Ltd in 2018

10 Orange Street
Sunnyside
Auckland Park 2092
South Africa
+2711 628 3200
www.jacana.co.za

© Jeremy Maggs, 2018
In association with Famous Faces Management
Visit win-book.co.za

ISBN 978-1-4314-2564-8

Cover design and layout by Shawn Paikin
Edited by Megan Mance
Proofread by Carla Wolber
Set in Minion Pro 11/15pt
Printed and bound by ABC Press, Cape Town
Job no. 003151

See a complete list of Jacana titles at www.jacana.co.za

Anne, Laura and Alex
Thanks for pushing me over the line

Contents

Foreword

Do not believe Jeremy Maggs when he says "I do not consider myself successful". He is wildly successful as perhaps the most recognisable television-media face in South Africa. Jeremy is the consummate professional in his field, a fearless interviewer and a model of how to do journalism in a complex country. So he was onto something when he decided to ask twenty other successful personalities to reveal the secrets of their success.

Prof Jonathan Jansen

This is a fascinating question that I too have grappled with over the years. Why do children in the same community or the same school or even the same family take such completely different routes in life? Why are some highly successful and others social dropouts even when they had the same opportunities? And why do some people with all the resources available to them become such spectacular failures in this journey called life? Such questions have been the subject of magazine speculation and serious research, for if we know what the key factors are that explain success, would we not be able to teach or train high achievers in a systematic manner?

It turns out that there is no one story that explains success. In fact, there are many routes to success. Some, like child stars, become instantly famous and are set for life in their careers and finances. Others, like myself, are late bloomers. As an old woman once encouraged me: "Not all kittens open their eyes on the same day." What a profound insight. And yet there are common markers of successful people.

Without exception, successful people work hard. Talent is not enough. You have to show up and deliver. These people work long hours and make huge sacrifices. Success is not like winning the lotto; there is no spontaneous or instant luck.

Successful people grab opportunities presented to them. Such opportunities might be few and far between but when chances come along, successful people take them. In a visit to the Free State university campus, one of the students asked Oprah Winfrey from the floor about the secret of her success. The answer was simple and profound: when the opportunity came, I took it.

We know that successful people hang around other successful people. The way to deal with peer pressure, I often tell young people, is to choose the right peers. I always chose people more ambitious and daring than me, peers I could look up to, who went further than me in their education. The converse is also true. Friends with low study or career goals tend to drag you down; you become like them in many cases.

Successful people, I have found, self-correct after failure. Here's the thing. You will fail. How you understand failure is the key. If failing for you means utter despair and the giving up on your goals, then that is your fate. But if failure is an opportunity for self-reflection and, more importantly, self-correction, then you learn from the fall and scale the wall that brought you down. Most people celebrate the success of another South African, Elon Musk, for sending rockets into space; what they do not talk about are the many rockets that exploded or landed in the ocean in the process of perfecting the successful launches that followed. Failure is nothing but opportunity to learn, which is why some people talk about failing forward.

Then there is this thing South Africans like to call "mindset". I cannot think of a better everyday word than "bloody-mindedness". It's that dogged determination to do well regardless of the circumstances. It's what happens when someone tells you that you can't but you make it your business to go out of your way and prove them wrong. Teachers, loved ones and even your closest friends can tell you what your limits are. Those with "bloody-mindedness" revel in proving the critics wrong. The examples I know among South Africans are endless – from the Down's syndrome child who became a qualified teacher to a heart-transplant patient who wins medals in the World Transplant games.

Successful people, in other words, respond well to a culture of high expectations. This is, in fact, a counter-cultural idea. Our school system sets pass marks at thirty and forty per cent and even passed a whole grade on a national level (Grade 8) with a condoned passing standard of twenty per cent in a recent academic year. I do not care what the reasons might be for such folly, but the messaging system from these policy actions to young South Africans is a simple and devastating one – we do not expect much from you. On this fact the educational research is unequivocal: in a culture of high expectations, students respond positively to the challenge.

In Jeremy Maggs's excellent collection of top-class South Africans you will find another characteristic of successful people. They are optimists. They really do believe that humans can become better people, that individuals can overcome their disabilities, that society can become more just. Being optimistic in a nation like South Africa right now is hard, I must confess, even for a diagnosed Pollyanna. The unrelenting crime, the dysfunctional schools, the captured state and the stubborn inequalities can bring anyone down. And then you see in almost every profession those who leap out of bed in the morning to make a difference in public health, early childhood education, prisoner rehabilitation and more. A man who made a huge difference in my childhood was given broken boxes and loose planks by farmers; he mended those boxes one by one and made a roaring business selling them back to the farmers to pack their fruits and vegetables. Where others saw brokenness, this optimistic man saw the potential for wholeness and successfully raised eight children to adulthood in a family of ten persons in a Cape Flats home.

Successful people have mentors. These are people you look up to for wisdom, guidance and correction along the journey of life. Some have more than one mentor to include a spiritual mentor alongside, say, a careers mentor. But they often lean on older and more experienced persons who can point the way to ideas, resources, networks and opportunities. There is no such thing as a self-made person. No student graduates without a host of relatives and friends who carried them through, especially during difficult periods. No chief executive gets to the top through sheer personal application. We depend on others. Successful people often seek out and find mentors who play traffic cop in that busy intersection called life.

I have also noticed that successful people are restless. They are always on the lookout for opportunities, for the next big break. Such people are not satisfied with their lot, they are certainly not fatalists. Truth is, opportunities do not come to you; you need to seek them out. A Nobel Laureate in physics or medicine would work for decades on a complex problem; what keeps them going is a sense of curiosity that simply will not go away. This intellectual restlessness is what eventually provides the breakthrough for the technology specialist working on an app that waters your plants at home while you are on holiday abroad. It was one of the world's most famous technology boffins who coined the restless phrase: "what's the next big thing?"

What this fresh and innovative book project of Jeremy Maggs offers is the embodiment of these principles in the real-life stories of twenty remarkable South Africans. This is not textbook content on what makes people successful; here we can witness how success works in the lives of people. In these trying times in our country, this inspirational book could not have come at a better time, for it makes hope real through the exceptional lives of otherwise ordinary people.

Jonathan D Jansen
Distinguished Professor in Education
University of Stellenbosch

Acknowledgements

Many years ago, I interviewed the well-groomed, best-selling fiction author Ken Follett during a global promotional tour. He elegantly swatted away my line of questioning about book-writing being a solitary effort.

Utter nonsense, he said. Apart from those directly involved with aspects like editing and research, family and friends also feel your pain. Many have not only felt my pain during this project but have also dealt with me being a complete pain in the neck. My project partner, Stuart Lee from Famous Faces Management, has pushed, cajoled and encouraged every step of the way. It is much appreciated. It was also his idea; as was the idea to turn the book into a corporate and conference presentation. And he took the photographs.

Stuart Lee

Win!

Every interview was done on camera in a pristine, well-lit environment and shot by Andy and Caroline Cook – two friends in the media business I've worked with for years. Many of the smartest and most unexpected questions came from Andy, who not only trained a gimlet eye on his subject but listened closely. Caroline's gentle ways made sure our interviewees didn't feel as if they were on an edition of the BBC's *Hard Talk*. Television is not only a time-consuming business but also people intensive. Producer colleagues Helene Nieuwenhuis, Yashini Padayachee, Celeste Phillips and Michelle Zietsman have been nothing but supportive and encouraging, as has eNCA's head of anchors, Sally Burdett, who would ask from time to time in the middle of news madness how things were coming on; and whether I needed a light snack. Badly, and yes, were my answers most of the time.

My immense thanks to the folk at Jacana, particularly Nadia Goetham, Megan Mance and Bridget Impey who tried (unsuccessfully, I think) to show me the difference between fast-paced journalism and authorship. At my first meeting with Megan, she politely inquired why I had an aversion to using paragraphs! I come from a hugely competitive immediate family. My wife Anne is an artist and author, elder daughter Laura an award-winning copywriter, and Alexandra a creative power-house and adventurous traveller. While their encouragement has been inspiring, none has been afraid to point out mistakes, like spelling, grammar and paragraphs! All of you are winners in your own right.

Caroline and Andy Cook

INTRODUCTION
The back story

At the outset let me say I don't consider myself successful. Far from it. Not a complete failure should we all meet one day in a conference room to run a comprehensive life-performance audit, but nothing like we imagine we'll be in our bulletproof twenties, high-energy ambition-driven thirties, and even our forties, when optimism is tempered by a degree of reality and responsibility. If there was a tangible success-measurement ladder placed against a high-rise building, I would be some steps up from the bottom rung and probably happy to end up somewhere in the middle when work finally starts to slow down and a small beach house beckons.

Can't be true, you scoff. People know him. He has a public profile. The man has tens of thousands of Twitter followers. He is a brand. He's met Oprah. I really did and she was scary, intense and inspiring all in sixty seconds.

Trust me, appearing on television every day (me that is), having people come and shake your hand, getting easier airline upgrades and quick restaurant reservations is no indication of real success. And that finally-off-my-chest admission was in part the genesis for a year-long quest in determining what real success is; how it is achieved and if it was possible in my late middle age to get me some!

In a broadcasting career that has spanned over thirty years, I've been lucky to have had a front seat watching the grand South African democracy show play out and to have interviewed many of the lead actors. All have been famous, some notorious, one or two slimy enough to make you want to want to reach for a wet wipe after shaking their hand and a few supercharged with magnetism and inspiration.

My first big radio interview was with a beaming Archbishop Emeritus Desmond Tutu, full of energy and optimism after the 1994 transition. At one stage, while in full ecumenical cry, espousing the miracle of nationhood and multi-coloured rainbows he leant across the table, scattered my notes and held both my hands to emphasise a point. I instantly felt an electric charge run through my entire body. At the end of the programme I quietly mentioned this to him and asked what had happened. "If you don't know, my son, one day you will." And then with a swirl of his purple cassock he waded into a photo-opportunity scrum and even when his diminutive figure was out of sight you knew exactly where he was because of that high-pitched cackle of a laugh that should be trademarked.

At the time I didn't know it, but the Arch and that interview started seeding an interest in the key drivers of success. Looking back at a crumpled set of notes, one question I saw I had asked him was how he had struggled to stay focused on a job when all around him the world seemed to be collapsing. Apart from his supreme faith in a higher power, he also spoke about acknowledging an unwavering faith in one's own ability to get the job done. Many other people you will read about in this book have told me the same thing.

Now you need to know at the outset that this is not a political book. With two exceptions, I've deliberately steered away from inviting political figures to participate in what has been a series of extended interviews on the nature and sustainability of success. Over the years I have encountered many politicians. Some I have liked, many I have and continue to loathe. There is much truth in that hoary old chestnut that asks how you know when a politician is lying. Their lips are moving. The late Helen Suzman told a very young version of me, in an interview in the tumultuous late eighties in the blood-soaked Eastern Cape, always to interrogate forensically what a politician was saying – even herself – as agendas and motives were inevitably opaque with self-interest and personal success and ambition always at the heart of it.

All politicians, she noted, have a ruthless streak. To a greater or lesser extent that is also a marker of success. But while the word ruthless is unfair to all of the guests between these pages, the word resolute is not. You'll observe that all are single-minded in their pursuit of goals, however big or small. So, while just two politicians participated in this project, others I have encountered are worth referencing when it comes to success.

I first encountered Jacob Zuma in a radio interview more than a decade ago when, as Deputy President and long before his litany of capture and no-confidence troubles, he played a significant role in the Great Lakes peace process. How, I asked him in a crackly telephone interview, did he lead the process and not lose his rag with recalcitrant parties. "My brother" – he's always been a master at personalising an encounter – "you have to listen more than you speak." He said the same thing to me after his ouster of President Mbeki in Polokwane to the obvious first-priorities question. "I plan to act only when I have listened and consulted." Let's leave Mr Zuma there shall we? There are real questions about who he has listened to and consulted with.

After the British Prime Minister Tony Blair was hoofed out of office, he visited South Africa on what I assume was a well-paid speaking trip and here was another famous person all mic'd up and ready to talk to me. At the time he was the whipping boy – as he remains today – of vocal Palestinian groups angry at his eager participation in the Iraq war. While that dominated a somewhat insincere interview, I did manage to slip in the burden of leadership question when it came to making big life-altering decisions. While the answer was pretty much stock-standard about loneliness at the top and clarity and certainty at a point in time which might change in hindsight, he was right – and others have told me the same thing – that success and leadership are about making tough calls rather than avoiding them.

I worked for a newspaper editor once whose strategy was to never make a decision in the hope that the issue would simply go away. He called it management by inertia and was proud of his ability to do nothing in the face of crisis. Needless to say, he didn't last long in the job.

Every single person in this book speaks about clear decision-making as a key component to achieving success. And to a person we have all grappled with the concept. Those who appear in this book are, on the surface of it, an eclectic bunch and there are obvious omissions. So here's how I did it in conjunction with Stuart Lee. He came up with the idea when we were once discussing the correlation between success and money. It was spurred by a television quiz show I hosted at the turn of the century, *Who Wants to be a Millionaire?*, where vast amounts of money were awarded to contestants who, under immense pressure, gave the right answer to tricky multiple-choice questions. Our conversation meandered onto successful people I had encountered in my broadcast career and if there was perhaps a common thread among them. And you are reading the result.

The participants are all inspiring people who I have personally met at some point, interviewed, and then admired not only for their success but for their hard work, commitment, tenacity and a common decency that runs through all of them.

The initial idea was to develop a template of twenty questions to be put to all the interviewees. The list of questions was easy enough to come up with but an interviewer is trained to listen to answers that hopefully take strange and intriguing tangents. So that rigid idea was scrapped after the first conversation and we went where our will wanted us to go. The interviews were done on camera and form the basis of a compelling talk that is designed to inspire and motivate South Africans to once again start reaching for their dreams and realising their full potential.

At the time of writing this backstory, I was simultaneously preparing for a TV interview on a study that claimed that, since the dawn of democracy, depression among all of us in South Africa had risen by close to sixty per cent. That is an alarming figure because when you are anxious, worried, concerned and debilitated, success is far more difficult, even impossible, to attain. Achieving success is also no walk in the park. These stories do not form part of a programme that certain basic tenets and rules will automatically bring you success. Far from it.

Given the sacrifice, diligence, application and tenacity my guests have shown, you will probably want to lie down in a dark room and question your existence. But it might just give you a single idea or thought-spark that will enable you to change a small part of your life. If that happens, then part of my job would be done.

By the way, since speaking to this array of stellar South Africans, I have not become instantly successful. Sadly. My position on that ladder remains much where it was. What I can say with confidence though is that I have renewed energy to look upwards and lift a foot. I hope you can get a firmer grip on your life ladder and also take a few steps. We might see each other on the way.

Cheryl Carolus

Wanna be successful?
Visit a hardware store

*T*his is the success story of a committed South African activist, politician, diplomat and business leader who once a year deep-cleanses her life by deleting people in her address book who add no value, optimism or inspiration. In a swirl of noise and energy, Cheryl Carolus arrives twenty minutes late and immediately owns the room, kissing everybody, shaking hands, ordering coffee and inquiring about collective general health in one long jumbled high-octane sentence. By way of excuse she says she's been cajoling politicians to, in her words, "grow a pair" and do something about the parlous state of both the country and the economy. It's easy to forgive this transgression of tardiness in the interests of affairs of state.

She dives straight into her favourite topic – the country – before I can even seed the conversation, saying she's an eternal optimist but is deeply concerned about how systemically and deeply the rot is entrenched.

"Something has gone wrong with the soul of this nation and I think we've all let it go on for too long. For middle-class people it's actually fine because we've privatised our safety and security with our response units; we've privatised our children's school care, sending them to private institutions, schools; we've privatised our healthcare with the fabulous health plans we have and so our tolerance level for what nonsense we're prepared to put up with actually just keeps on shifting out.

"But what's been great has been this nuclear action of President Zuma leaving us under such a cloud it has jolted people to want to seize back power. I sense right now there's a much stronger sense of civil society rejuvenating itself. Now it's a question of how we make an impact on my organisation, the ANC, and actually get members to understand they should not take voters for granted."

I decide to let this high-speed political spinnaker run a little longer before we get to the notion of success.

So what does all of this political negativity mean as a portent for the next couple of years and does she still hold on to the optimism she's held for so long in her life?

"I don't think we're going to be out of the woods fully, even when President Zuma is gone. It's about the values on which the next set of leaders in the ANC are going to be elected. I think it's going to be turbulent and messy. This boil is so big and there's so much filth around it we're going to have to cut deep and lance it quite clinically."

I see an opportunity for a clever segue here before we get too physiological. What should successful people be doing in times like this when there is so much turbulence? What responsibilities do we all have?

Cheryl, not missing a beat or drawing breath, says it's about the P-word. Power.

"People like you and me have power to make and influence change. The big mistake we've made since democracy dawned is we think only the State has the power to mess us around, to make us happy, to look after us. Not at all. We have that power. We have to use it."

Let's move away from politics and on to the pure nature of success and its attainment. She believes success is nothing if you're not respected by your peers, by your family and by your community. And part of being successful, she says, is being able to rise and lift others with you at the same time.

"If you are successful in a sea of misery and depravation, you are always at risk, so I attach a lot of value to helping other people succeed in business."

Cheryl then throws down a challenge to other successful people, saying they should make it one of their missions to expand their ecosystems.

"And one of the primary parts of anyone's ecosystem is that it's not just about your business but your family and your community. You can make a huge difference sometimes by doing very small things."

Cheryl also believes there is a moral dimension to success and that it's not only wrong to trample over others, but stupid, because the more successful other people are, the more successful your country and your ecosystem become.

Phew. Let's take a breath here and gather our thoughts. And no one has even taken an initial sip of coffee. This conversation is like a sprint finish at the Tour de France. Maybe a quick tale of when it first dawned on her that she had achieved a modicum of accomplishment?

"Undoubtedly, when I became High Commissioner in the UK and the over-reaction of my mother. She was always proud of my struggle roles; of the fact I was recognised as a leader in the UDF and later in the ANC and that even Nelson Mandela respected me, but when I went to London, she said, 'I wish your grandmother was alive to see how far you've come. You are now a proper person in the Queen's country!'"

Much like HRH, Cheryl has had her fair share of hard times. So how do you overcome adversity?

"It's about one's ability to be resilient and to keep rewriting one's script because we all should have some sort of plan and thread for our life. For me it is a generosity that starts with being kind to yourself but also being brutally honest as to when I'm not succeeding or where I have failed."

She says it's about having a complete sense of self-worth and telling yourself that success is deserved. "I tell myself I am a worthy, capable person and I have confidence in myself to say when something is not working and being able to be honest about it."

A lot of this introspection happens when Cheryl is in her PJs. "The older I get, the more value I attach to my sleeping patterns and when

I no longer wake up at two in the morning in a cold sweat and think about what I'm doing, or say why on earth did I think I could pull this one off, then I know it's time to move on. I also love the fact that at this life-stage I am a serial re-inventor of myself, confident that I have a set of core skills and accomplishments that I'm recognised for."

So back to that cold-sweat thing. When it comes in the middle of the night, what's it all about? In Cheryl's case it's not being healthy enough to chase the things she still wants to chase. In this year-long quest for the secrets of success, time and time again I've been told how important the chase is, but with it, the fear of not having the capability to run.

Like many others Cheryl takes good care of herself. "Some people don't think so because they think I eat too much chocolate or drink too much red wine." Who am I to judge one's indulgences, being highly partial to a little Merlot and Lindt myself.

Successful people, it seems, also have set rituals that continually re-spin their flywheel. In Cheryl's case it's on her birthday. "Every year I get up at 5 am to do a personal balance sheet. I look at my toxic liabilities and delete people's numbers from my cellphone. You'll get deleted if you are a horrible person; somebody who does bad things to me and other people. I simply have no room for people like that in my life. Those who hurt others and who try to hurt me." I'm glad to say I'm still in Cheryl's contacts list!

She believes de-cluttering is a healthy part of life, both emotionally and workwise. But there's more. Patently it's a busy birthday before gifts are opened and cake is cut. She also draws up a list of people she thinks she needs to apologise to for any transgressions committed over the past twelve months. "Apology, I think, is something that successful people should become better at because we are often surrounded by people whose importance we underplay in our lives."

By 5 pm Cheryl says she's drinking bubbles but not before setting goals for the next hectic year. "I am officially an ambitious person. I love success – I thrive on success – and I think most human beings do. I love it when a thing comes together, particularly when it is totally impossible. In fact, the most attractive thing to me is if somebody says this thing looks impossible. I love getting to the top of huge mountains."

So in order to scale these mountains it's fair to say that you have to stay competitive most or all of the time. How, then, does this always-at-full-speed dynamo do that? She goes to hardware stores. "I love learning new stuff all the time. It gives me the edge. Don't put me in a Builders Warehouse. I look at everything and ask how does it work and then I buy it, battle to assemble it and try and use it." In this year-long quest for the secret formula for success, the route has been paved with many clichés and none more so than that old line of pushing through the tough times. But in Cheryl's case it has resonance.

"It not only takes consistent hard work but also being on the right side of an issue. Apartheid was a very bad idea and I think early on people had to decide which the winning side was. I and many others took it."

In our energetic conversation Cheryl also coins a new word – "enoughness". She says, like most people, she likes having enough money to indulge herself. "But I don't feel I need a handbag that costs a hundred-and-twenty-five thousand rand and I say this as a girl with a formidable handbag collection. I also like wearing nice clothes, but will I spend a hundred thousand rand on an outfit? I think that's obscene. I don't define myself by my material possessions and anyone who wants to be seen on Facebook and Instagram wearing expensive stuff says they have a moral emptiness."

Like many other successful people, Cheryl admits to having a short attention span that she believes works to her advantage. "Give me an impossible thing to turn around or build and I will do it successfully. But ask me to maintain the momentum, I can't. Once I've achieved a turnaround I must leave or I will destroy the organisation."

It's a useful observation for people climbing that big shiny ambition ladder. Know when to leave. You will notice that one of the questions I've put to most of the guests in the pages of this book is the one about legacy. Cheryl has the answer down pat and I suspect she's been asked it before. "I want to be remembered for how business should get done in South Africa by somebody who was given opportunities in the BEE space. But also around the constitution and the rule. But the biggest legacy I want to be part of was my small role in ending apartheid and the bigotry that went with it. I have the scars on my back and I carry them as a badge of honour. I'm also grateful I'm young enough to be part of actively rebuilding a different future."

Takeaways

Success is being able to rise and lift others with you at the same time.

Success is having a complete sense of self-worth and telling yourself it's deserved.

Successful people should become better at apologising because they are surrounded by people whose importance they underplay.

Adrian Gore

Predictability annoys me

*T*his is the success story of a man whose primary business mission in life has been to make South Africans healthier. Moments before our interview Adrian Gore tells me he did fifty push-ups in his office before running up the stairs. Given I'd had a good high-carb fry-up for breakfast after I'd put off gym and walking the dog for a fifth consecutive day, I felt slightly aggrieved, but let's press on. After all, I thought, this is a quest to uncover what makes the country's iconic health entrepreneur successful.

Before we get into our conversation, let me relate a personal anecdote. Every time Adrian presents Discovery's results he calls me in with a single remit – ask me the toughest and most brutal questions you can about anything to do with the numbers or the company. Hold nothing back. Come for me. He does this in front of his entire Exco who, given the company's robust and competitive culture, hold nothing back in criticism. Once this gladiatorial exercise is over, Adrian believes he can handle anything the most forensic of analysts or argumentative of journalists can throw at him. It's an awesome display of self-confidence that courses through his wiry frame. If I'm gushing a bit here, forgive me, I hold this man in the highest esteem.

So, I wonder if he has a definition of what a successful person is and whether he lives up to his own definition. He immediately throws me a curveball, saying the idea of success or reaching success is not something he's comfortable with.

"Of course I'm proud of what I've achieved and I get a sense that as a team we've built something that is amazing, but my sense of success is like the slope of a curve." You should know at this point that Gore is an actuary and I was waiting for mathematical analogy. I just didn't expect it to come so soon. "With me it doesn't matter where you are, it's what that slope looks like. I'd much rather be at the bottom on the way up – it feels better than being at the top sloping down. For me success is more about the gradient of a curve."

Adrian says he's highly sensitive to mediocrity and constantly needs that curve to be heading north. He goes on to say that he doesn't have a fear of failure, but rather a fear of mediocrity, a fear of not making an impact and a fear of the ordinary. Success, he believes, is entirely predicated on a sense of growth and constantly moving up his life curve.

I'm curious about his assertion that making an impact is important. "Impact means that in a social sense you're making a difference. I'm not sure it's a tangible, definable or even measurable thing but I think you feel when you're making a difference."

So what impact, then, does he believe he is making?

"We've made millions of people change their lives, globally. In our company in China we have a million people doing ten thousand steps a day. That is impact." Adrian fervently believes that staying fit and healthy is probably the key component to success. "If I can get sleep and stay fit, I'm highly productive; if not I'm relatively useless. I have a hell of a pressurised life. My wife had a baby at 50 so I'm changing nappies, and going through board reports at the same time, and the only antidote is staying fit and keeping the routine." It's worth pointing out here a delicious irony in Gore's iron-man existence. His father was a cigarette trader.

Part of Adrian's success has been on product innovation in the highly competitive financial services sector. So where, I wonder, do good ideas come from and once you have one how do you build on it? It's not as good a question as I thought.

"The good idea is the gold, the building-on and the execution is usually simple, provided you have the best brains and technology – which these days are something of a commodity. Of more importance – right at the beginning of the vision – is having in mind what the end is going to look like."

Adrian also believes successful people interrogate ideas and predicted outcomes a little more than, say, those of us who had bacon and eggs for breakfast instead of a kale and wheatgrass smoothie.

He says: "I'm a natural contrarian; I take nothing at face value. I always believe there's something bigger out there. I have this perpetually frustrated mindset and am always unsatisfied. I always think that I can do and be better."

So, I wonder, is a contrarian attitude critical to success? Adrian says: "I don't think it's necessarily important but it certainly describes me. I'm naturally suspicious of the road most travelled and I don't know why. It irritates me and I think it's genetic. Things that are predictable irritate me. It's a terrible thing. It makes you dissatisfied, but also makes you question things you know."

Adrian also believes that looking back at achievement is dangerous. He says that while it's important to learn from mistakes, it's more useful to look forward and ask how to scale the next curve. He also believes that with a lifetime of lessons learnt he has become less arrogant. So let me seize on that word – that self-description is the type that creates headlines. Was that important in the early days, then, to have a degree of hubris? A sense of superiority perhaps?

Adrian thinks it is. "If I think of myself as a youngster starting out in my twenties, I was incredibly arrogant, with a deep conviction about my own ability. I'm not sure how I behaved but I did have a single-minded belief. So, although it sounds unattractive, there is a need for ego if you're going to be successful."

But he quickly counters the argument citing the Icarus factor – the idiot who flew too close to the sun. "I think you need to use that energy in a positive way. If you start believing in yourself too much, the fall can be both hard and painful."

I shift the focus to goal-setting and in Adrian's case it's go big or go home. At Discovery he's set the 2018 company goal of being the best in the insurance category globally. "It's absolutely idiotic, right, I must be the only CEO who puts something that stupid in the public domain and many are going to hang me for that goal. That's fine, though – it's an amazingly powerful motivator but I can already feel the noose tightening around my neck."

He cites something called the Utility Prospect Theory, which, simplified, says potential loss is much more of a motivator than potential gain. This is how Adrian explains it: "If we set a goal, we've got something to lose and we are scared about it." Which then segues nicely into our next line of conversation. What does he fear?

And this answer, I suspect, separates the men from the boys. "I'm not a fearful person. Like most I'm concerned about the country's situation, but I see it as a time of huge opportunity. When people are distracted there are opportunities."

I always feel one can learn about successful people through their early childhood dreams – no teenager wants to be an actuary if in fact they know what it is. Adrian wanted to race motorcycles. "I was never good enough, though. I broke a few bones, but I was never able to make an impact." We've heard that word before, haven't we? "So I studied actuarial science because of the sheer challenge of it. I felt it would give me an entrée to rare opportunities, which I think it did. And then, amazingly, in insurance I found a world of unbelievable institutional power. I think my days at the Liberty Group gave me a sense of what an institution could achieve in the world."

Adrian, like so many other successful people, describes himself as pathologically competitive. "I just don't like losing, I'm obsessive about it. I can feel the competitive force in my genetic makeup."

And when you fail? "I'm actually not a bad loser and I never cut corners."

And in the blink of an eye he uses the word mediocrity again. So how does Adrian define it? "A kind of just normality. Getting home at four in the afternoon, the dog bringing you a paper from behind the picket fence. In a world that's changing it feels unfulfilling."

Part of his constant pursuit of success is staying professionally fresh. His advice is to embrace the most complex of problems with vigour and enthusiasm and appreciate them as growth opportunities. "Learning from others and learning from situations – given the vast world I'm exposed to – I find inspiring. It re-energises my ability."

Family time, Adrian believes, is a massive boost to individual success and he contends that positive brain chemistry is affected by feeling a sense of gratitude. Adrian also believes that successful people have a responsibility to inspire others. "Most people have a greatness in them and they should try to reveal that. It gets back to my deep belief about being a good leader. Your basic requirement is to inspire. If you can create a sense of inspiration, of positivity and vision for the team you lead, you're doing your job. You certainly don't have to be a genius, you don't have to be smarter and you don't have to know more technical stuff than everybody else."

Before he does another fifty push-ups and drinks the second of two strong espressos he allows himself every day, I ask about his relationship with money. It's no great secret that he has lots of it. Firstly, he says, he's not a trader. It's not in his nature and he's also not a great risk-taker with money. His parting shot is: "don't bet the house". He also exhorts us to think more positively about South Africa. It's worth repeating part of a seminal keynote speech he gave: "Because we are so focused on the negatives, we actually don't know the positives. We have to make it clear to the people we lead that there *is* great potential. The world is in fact becoming a better place yet we think it is getting worse."

He also urges South African business and political leaders to do a better job of setting goals for the country and for us all to recognise that huge progress continues to be made. "While it is important to acknowledge and tackle problems such as chronic unemployment and inequality in South Africa, huge advancements have been made in certain areas. These include advances in rolling-out the world's biggest anti-retroviral programme, surplus energy, millions being lifted out of poverty and an increase in life expectancy."

Like so many successful people, he doesn't linger once the interview is over. The focus is on the next meeting and how to achieve maximum impact.

Takeaways

Success is predicated on a sense of growth and constantly moving up life's curve.

Staying fit and healthy are probably the key components to success.

There is a need for ego if you're going to be successful.

Pravin Gordhan

Keep introducing sanity

*T*his is the success story of a giant of a man who, for the past two years, has been buffeted by stinging political forces that have not only impacted on his health, but also the well-being of his family. Yet throughout months of adversity, Pravin Gordhan has not wavered in sticking to and articulating deeply held principles of honour, decency and integrity. He is for many the epitome of success where he is humble about his accomplishments, self-deprecating at times but with a backbone of tungsten steel when it comes to speaking out about the ills of society and the travails of the planet.

We meet on the side-lines of yet another conference he has been invited to address, where delegates want to hear a combination of hard truth flavoured with optimism. They want a sage to tell them that it's going to be all right. He'll do that but not before telling them that being part of the leading one per cent in South Africa places a huge expectation on them. How they behave, how they treat their staff, how they need to be less greedy and how to become more active members of civil society.

Notwithstanding a longer view that we can get it right in South Africa, he tells me that the state of the country and the ANC keeps him awake at night.

"So many people have given their lives, their time, their energy and their potential over many years. But at the same time there is also the reassurance that we have done well in the past twenty-odd years, and we have a foundation that can't be cracked. We will, I know, be able to build on that foundation again."

If anyone has the right to be bleak, it's Pravin Gordhan. So what, I ask, drives the optimism?

"It's a long-standing and fundamental belief that we need a more just society. And as my understanding increased both politically and in terms of what social justice meant, that developed into a passion. But with passion also comes the question of how to achieve concrete results."

Pravin believes there are two key elements to achieving results.

"One is having a strategy to overcome obstacles and the second is to not lose one's sense of the goal and the principles that inform what we do."

Part of having a passion, I suggest, is the ability to fuel it. He says it's always about looking forward. "I have been one of those individuals who always looked at opportunities to do better, not in a personal sense but in an organisational sense."

He cites the South African Revenue Service that he ran for years where his driving dictum was asking why it could not be benchmarked against global institutions. As it turned out, he achieved that status. But more importantly, he says, people should have the humility to learn from others. Not to mimic them perfectly, but to adapt what you learn from them to your own circumstances.

On goal-setting, Gordhan cautions about over-reaching. You need to break down the challenge into bite-size chunks and become hyper-adaptable to your environment.

Let's tease that out a bit shall we? Pravin lists a couple of must-dos in this respect. Firstly, being open to your environment and being able to receive messages from the outside is important, because leaders often become preoccupied with themselves. He also says while dynamic people like to forge ahead, more progress is typically made by having the ability to work in groups.

"It is about a collective ethic in a sense. Although leaders must play an important role in catalysing or crystallising thinking, the thinking happens in the particular environment." But how does a leader find it within him or herself to listen, because often the more experience you have, the better you think you are at knowing everything?

It's about tempering arrogance, which he says is a dangerous phenomenon. Having said that, there is no mathematical formula. "Sometimes you might overstep the individual element, and other times you might understate it. But it is having an understanding that you need to build fluidity into your life."

"It's also useful," he says, "to take regular time out to reflect."

Given the default to group dynamics and staying true to principles of modesty, I know my next question on when he thought he had achieved success is going to solicit an answer full of twists and turns. And here it comes. "Success has never been part of my vocabulary but the feedback one gets is satisfying."

There must be a moment? Pravin returns to his struggle and activist days, saying when he'd mobilised large numbers of people around a campaign, even if only a partial victory was obtained, it was about as good as it got.

We'll settle for that and I think it's fair to say that he must be feeling somewhat pleased nowadays as his de facto position as the country's anti-graft godfather has catapulted him to near mystical status. He probably won't like that description but I am prepared to argue it. Preferably not in court though – he has a habit of winning.

Pravin admits to feeling a sense of accomplishment both as Finance Minister (twice) and head of the SA Revenue Service. "It was validating because I got to see people and machinery grow and with that came respect from the public."

Pravin also takes the opportunity to open up, albeit guardedly, about his recent travails through 2017 and what some say has been South Africa's most testing time post-democracy. He's been at the vanguard of the fight against state capture and he's come in for a battering. He says he does wake up some mornings and ask how much longer he can carry on at the pace that has consumed his life. To that end he says successful people need a micro-world.

"I am privileged to have a supportive family and comrades and friends who are honest souls who want to bring about real and important change – both within the ANC and within the government itself. That keeps me motivated."

He says he is touched and moved whenever he walks into a shop or a garage and experiences the level of political understanding in the country and what and who is right – and what is wrong.

For a man who sets a pace that would challenge and shame people half his age, Pravin says downtime has become critical and he urges those who can, to decompress. He takes time out late in the evening to relax and flip through news channels. Spot the irony. He describes time with his family as important recovery moments.

I was told once by another leader I admire, Peter Matlare, when I worked for him in the broadcast environment, that he was also paid to stare out the window. Being the gung-ho fellow that I am, I dismissed PG's exhortation to introspection as a sign of weakness. He thinks it's critical to spend quality time thinking.

"Keep reflecting, keep asking questions and listen to others."

He also confesses to being something of a magpie when colleagues and friends send him articles and clippings. But it all informs a bigger dynamic, which he says enables him to refresh the answer to questions such as: What is going on in the world today? What are the new dynamics that are unfolding? What do those dynamics mean for new trends that might actually be developed? Where are we in this country at this point in time? What are the new complexities that we actually have to deal with? An impressive list – and there am I more than happy to binge-watch *House of Cards* or read the new Ken Follett thriller.

Apart from Nelson Mandela, Pravin surprises me with the person he looks up to. While he's not a Catholic and not even religious, he admires Pope Francis for re-introducing sanity and contesting well-accepted norms of consumerism, individualism, greed and of relentless accumulation.

We get into a hard political critique about South Africa's body politic when I ask him if he has broken rules in his life.

"In the old days you had to break rules in order to make new ones. More recently we were lectured by President Zuma about how we should exercise 'the ANC conscience', which is prescribed in its constitution. It says very clearly: contribute to non-racial unity and non-sexism; contribute to social and economic development for all South Africans and transform the economy. He breaks all the rules."

Pravin dismisses the legacy question with what I think is a little contempt. "Legacy is built into what you do at a day-to-day level. If you do it well you will be remembered for it. If you have done it badly, you will be remembered for that as well."

And so, with an audience waiting in the next room, I ask if, in 2018, South Africa is going to be a better place.

"I am hopeful it is, and that is where optimism comes in. But at the same time that is where the realism comes in as well. Nothing in South Africa, or indeed the rest of the world, is going to emerge without a contest; without some level of struggle. Those battles will have to be fought and there is no guarantee you are going to win. The only question is how much destruction and loss of opportunity, and loss of benefit to the majority of South Africans that we are here to serve, has resulted in in this dip in our fortunes. And that is the regrettable part of where we are heading. But at the end of it all, as long as you are part of the struggle – this new struggle where we all need to be alive, aware, vigilant, engaged and involved."

As we pack up and Pravin leaves us, a spontaneous and tumultuous applause erupts from the room next door. The man is a rock star.

Takeaways

Success is about looking forward but also about spending quality time thinking.

Successful people should have the humility to learn from others.

Success means being open to your environment and being able to receive messages from the outside.

Jabu Mabuza

Successful people rewrite the rules

*T*his is the success story of a man who, some years ago, you might have looked at askance and possibly waved a fist at, and tooted your horn. Loudly. But had you had an opportunity to stop and engage him, chances are you would have been won over quickly. He's one of those individuals who not only owns the room he walks into with a kinetic abundance of bonhomie and goodwill, but in time might also make an offer to buy it.

Jabulani (Jabu) Mabuza, who started out as a taxi driver, is a highly respected business leader, entrepreneur, facilitator and wearer of fine fedora hats that have become something of a trademark. Latterly he's best known for his role as chairman of Telkom, but has spent time overseeing two big hotel groups and SA Tourism. He's also a leading and outspoken voice in the SA business community as part of Business Unity South Africa. He has the close ear of most in the cabinet and has been known in the past, while not quite reading the riot act, to certainly cause enough noise and disruption to make things uncomfortable.

He is, should you ever be so lucky to be invited, an over-attentive host at an international rugby match suite and I'd suggest you take an Uber ride back. I suppose you can take the man out of the hospitality industry ... but, well you know how the old line goes.

We sit down in the offices of his newest venture – an investment holding company – around a boardroom table the size of an aircraft carrier. Apart from my younger daughter, he's the only person I know who calls me Jezza.

He's another in this series of conversations who is surprisingly demure in describing his own success. "I see myself as a person who has only made a contribution. If I have tried ten things, at least six have been successful – so I still believe there is a long road to go."

And then Jabu goes a little biblical on me. "The paths I have chosen have been filled with many valleys and hills. So I might go down and never come up, or I might go up and never come down. So to say, I think success is an end state, a destination and I don't think I have reached it yet."

So it would seem then that making a contribution to society is emblematic of success? Jabu provides a simple formula in answer: "We tend to make business look more complicated than it is. Business is simply about people who both produce and consume. So when I say I have had a good day in the shop, it is because I have sold more than I hoped I would."

And part of it, suggests Jabu, is having a deep understanding of the human psyche in this equation. "The minute we spend more time understanding people, and not in a patronising or condescending way, the more successful we will become."

And here is a valuable little vignette. Jabu suggests the most important part of any business relationship is remembering a person's name. Now the Jezza makes sense. It makes me feel special and singled out.

The more balls you have up in the air, and I speak as one who battles to keep one up, I imagine it becomes more difficult to stay focused and engaged. Jabu says he's not a great sit-down-and-plan person, but every endeavour he tackles is done with a high degree of focus. "I take the things I do seriously; I take my job seriously; I take the people I am engaged with seriously; I take their issues as my issues."

And it's the final point that may be the most important. "I stay engaged in recognising that all people have got aspirations and fears in the same way that I have. See yourself in the other person and you will stay focused."

But there is an interesting counterpoint here. Jabu says that while it's fine to pursue excellence, just don't take yourself too seriously. That, he says, is the highest level of vanity, and the moment it becomes about you is the moment you lose the plot.

Jabu is one of a handful of people I spoke to who says luck has played a huge part in his success. But it's about having the talent not only to see it when it jumps out in front of you, but the ability to seize it – and to seize it quickly. A chance meeting for a matter of moments could change your life. The advice here is grab it and don't stand back.

He recounts one of his first meetings with Meyer Khan, the legendary boss of South African Breweries, as it was known at the time. "He said to me, 'You seem to be a man among men; you have got balls; I want to have a beer with you.'" You need to have courage to follow through and then after that it's all about hard graft."

Jabu is now chairing the South African division of Anheuser-Busch InBev, the new merged company with SAB Miller. While Jabu has been talking, I've been processing the hills-and-valleys analogy and I'm trying to work out where in deep middle age I find myself. The idea, of course, is to get out of that valley and find the sunshine as quickly as possible. So many of us tend to live in a world of professional shade. How do you push through and find the right path? It's about constant engagement with what is around you.

Says Jabu: "You have to keep learning about the environment in which you operate, internalise the issues of the people you are dealing with and through that they give you confidence to continue."

Our conversation meanders into failures in his stellar career path and lessons learnt from a father who seemed to have Victorian principles. "I was expelled from school in 1977 for my involvement in the 1976 uprising and disowned by my father who caught me drunk. He said I could 'never ever again call yourself my son.'" A young Jabu prevailed on the kindness of a cousin who paid his school fees from part of her medical bursary. He passed matric and, as he puts it, was "Daddy's boy" again.

Some months later he was confronted with a dilemma that many in the 1970s might have faced. Political conviction was telling him to take a train to Swaziland and into exile as his father's retrenchment put the onus of earning a living for his family squarely on his shoulders. And that's how he ended up driving a taxi and eventually how he met a coterie of enlightened South Africans who recognised his potential. Part of that potential was Jabu's negotiating skills and with that, the ability to finesse and seal the deal.

What is more important then, chasing the deal or signing it? I sense it's all about the work and not necessarily the result. Jabu again references his mentor Meyer Khan who told him never to appear too keen in the early stages of negotiation and that there is nothing wrong in business in faking one's intentions; life lessons for Jabu.

Our conversation now arrives at money and the accumulation of wealth. Jabu did set himself a gain target, which he says is a useful tool to provide focus. He reached that goal some years ago. It was a large one and my inherent sense of decency prevents me from disclosing it, but here's one piece of excellent advice. Jabu says negotiate carefully and wisely and don't be embarrassed to be confident about your own worth to a company or a project. He proclaims that he always feels he is not paid enough for the contribution that he makes.

Jabu says, somewhat ruefully, that he's never found the absolute secret to a work-life balance and works as many hours as it takes to get the job done. Back to that Victorian father of his. "Unfortunately my father put something in my head a long time ago, which still troubles me. He said as long as people believe you can still do something, you will do it. For as long as you run out of time, you will cut down on your sleeping time. I am also fortunate that I've never had a nagging and whinging wife. My wife would rather have me happy at the golf course, than sulking behind the TV screen at home with her."

In South Africa in recent years, business and politics have become inextricably linked and Jabu finds himself at the complicated nexus of where the two meet. He has become one of the de facto faces of South African business and its increasing concern over where the nation is heading, its ability to live up to its original post-democracy promises and how that impacts on all of our efforts to be successful.

"I am extremely worried about this country. But I also am encouraged about the resilience of our people. Their fighting spirit and the fact that you can't push us beyond a particular point. I think South Africans have reached that point where we are saying 'here and no further'. We are at the edge. But in our recent history we have spent a lot of time looking down that gorge and gingerly working our way back up."

So what are the chances of making it back up the steep incline? And here's a parting shot that should inspire most. At a recent university graduation ceremony where he was conferred with an honorary doctorate, Jabu had this to say to a hall of sparkling-eyed graduates: "As you launch into your careers, please don't get weighed-down by populism or pessimism. Care about people. And make your impact on our country and the world a positive one. Those values, of 'please', 'I am sorry' and 'thanks' will see you through."

The French have a magnificent saying *L'esprit de l'escalier* or "staircase wit". It's that terrible feeling when you get home and only then come up with the perfect retort, insult or question. I should have asked Jabu then and there if he saw a new career in politics. I didn't, but it wouldn't surprise me if there was.

Takeaways

Success is spending more time working on understanding people.

Success is about remembering people's names.

Successful people negotiate carefully and are not embarrassed about their worth to a company or project.

Wendy Lucas-Bull

Never be the naysayer

This is the success story of a South African corporate giant who has made gender parity in the workplace a driving mission during her professional life. Part of the drive was a bizarre policy when she was made partner at a global consulting firm that women like her in an exalted senior role could only have one pregnancy. Wendy Lucas-Bull, chair of Barclays Africa and founder of the Peotona Group – which, by the way, includes among its luminaries another star among these pages; Cheryl Carolus – has three sons. Right back at them.

She changed that absurd policy pretty darn quickly. Apart from mentorship, female empowerment, standing up for herself and righting wrongs, Wendy is also a big proponent of getting corporate culture just right. She defaults to the pillars of African leadership theory – humanity, collaboration, trust, respect and courage. You'll also know it as Ubuntu.

On the day of our discussion she arrives late, because she couldn't find a parking spot in the downstairs basement of the Sandton offices of the company she chairs. You would have thought she might have a reserved space, wouldn't you?

It's a silly thing like no favouritism that I think defines her. As you're about to discover, that streak of humility is a driving force.

She defines success as making a meaningful difference to other people's lives. "It's what has driven me from day one, even from when I was a teenager, really, was to actually make a difference."

And the reason? "It makes me feel worthwhile. What is the point of being alive if you're not going to make a difference?"

This seems a statement worth delving into. Making a difference can be a fairly amorphous thing. Is it making a difference; making sure that people have an easier life? Is it uplifting people? Is it making people happy? She says it's about using her skill set to make a contribution in the best way she can. "I mentor many young people so it's about seeing them grasp the opportunities they can just with a little bit of air under their wings. It's not making things happen for them because they have to do it themselves but it's about helping to guide them with decisions and thinking through things."

We enter an interesting realm here as Wendy says she uses her extensive network of contacts built over the years to help light the career flame. It's an important point she raises. The more successful someone becomes, the more people they draw into their orbit and the more you get drawn into theirs. It's a question of positively managing those relationships and leveraging them when you have to.

What, I ask, makes a good mentor, because in a society such as South Africa I would contend that those who have become successful have a moral obligation to help harness others? Wendy says: "Someone who is able to listen properly, understand the context an individual is coming from and then appreciate what they are dealing with through their eyes rather than through yours. It's not about giving them the answers and not about lecturing them but about helping them think things through so that they end up with a pathway that is right for them, right for their personality, right for the skills that they've got at that particular time and also helping to connect them."

Part of Wendy's commitment to mentorship is that it seems it was a missing piece in her life. She recalls the start of her professional life in an audit and consulting firm where she was only the fourth woman among thousands of international partners. She was also the youngest. She describes her time there as being lonely. "I had to demonstrate more competence, more resilience, more courage than any male counterpart would have done. The bar was always higher."

Part of Wendy's drive to the top was acknowledging an ambitious nature fuelled by a passion for competitive sport – tennis, high board diving, hockey, squash and gymnastics. You would think with that type of extra-mural schedule Wendy would be a precise goal setter. "Not at all and my advice to younger people would be not to become too obsessed with goals. I took every opportunity pretty much as it came. Maybe if you have big goals you set your sights on one thing and you miss a whole lot of opportunities that may come your way."

So many of us in life have the potential to seize opportunity but miss it because we're either fearful or we don't spot the chance. How do you get that right? "It's about looking closely at what your skills are. It would be foolhardy to step into something where you have no competence or context in order to play in that space. It's about picking the spaces where you've got that right and then backing yourself to the hilt and appreciating that with the task there will be stress."

Wendy says she is also a risk taker but using the competence and context measure she seems to have got it right. Wendy cautions those on the ladder to greatness to pause a while when they can.

"I have a big capacity to get through stuff and when I need to I get through volumes. But I absolutely take time out for myself and my family. Family is a big leveller. When your kids are small it's non-negotiable in terms of the attention they need when you get home. I have always spent appropriate time with my children. So when I'm present I'm fully present and when I've got a task to finish I put my head down and finish it and then when it's family time and switch-off time I can actually switch off completely."

I then ask Wendy to find a couple of personal brand descriptors. She starts with that important but slightly over-traded word resilience but also fearlessness. She was given a plaque or an award once from FNB staff with the inscription Captain Fearless. I sense she likes that. Part of her success, it seems, is an ability to bring her A-game to the table. Or, as you're about to read, a hiking holiday.

"A year ago I went on the gorilla hiking pilgrimage with all of my sons. The first day was eight hours long and the second seven. I slipped in the first half hour of the second day; walked on and I didn't realise I had serious fractures until I got home. But I was there to do something, complete a task and nothing was going to deter me." Like I said, resilience. But also courage and toughing it out.

Throughout their careers many successful people have to deal with conflict. Wendy agrees, but suggests a better way. The first point being her favourite word – context. In other words, understand the different dynamics to the problem before wading in. Like I would! She then suggests trying to unbundle the issue by starting at the conclusion and working backwards and dissecting opinions and assumptions.

Like many people in her rarefied corporate world, Wendy admits to making mistakes. But she says it's the swift recovery that is more important. "It's about retaining sufficient humility and admitting you don't know all the answers. But when it comes to making big decisions you have to back yourself, be decisive and make a call. You also have to put in place sufficient measures to say what are going to be the indicators of success. You then place checkpoints to check your assumptions and if your assumptions along the timeline prove to be out of position then you have to change tack."

It's excellent advice – developing a step-by-step checks-and-balances methodology so the mistake doesn't surprise you at the end. You can see it coming.

Wendy's big mistakes, interestingly, are not deals that have gone sour or under-estimating cost and risk. Rather they have to do with the human element. "My mistakes have come in underestimating or misjudging people in terms of their values and overestimating people's competence." And she candidly admits they are mistakes that she not only makes time and time again but that they are necessary to make. Huh?

"You don't want to be the person in the room with all the negative energy looking for what's wrong. I'm happy to make those mistakes and not be the naysayer all the time."

Intermittently in this project we've asked people who they look up to. Someone who inspires them and from whom they draw energy and fortitude. Without hesitation Wendy calls out the embattled former finance minister Pravin Gordhan. "He's got courage, integrity and cares deeply about not only the country but about making it better for other people." She says the thing that she most admires is the high bar he has set for himself, something that others wishing to succeed also need to do.

Success, it seems is a life of no compromise. Before she has to move her car from the basement I thought it might be useful to return to the gorillas and the type of lessons she might have picked up from these incredibly sophisticated and sensitive primates. She cites a visceral feeling of wisdom exuding from a single silver-back she came close to. I think it takes one to recognise another – with maturity and experience life's hard knocks translate into wisdom. The problem is so many of us don't know how to use it and impart it. Wendy is one of those people who runs counter to that observation. She recognises that her dedication and hard work have paid off but that they mean nothing unless they are paid forward.

Takeaways

Successful people know they want to make
a difference.

Successful people are not too obsessed with goals.

Success is about retaining sufficient humility and
admitting you don't know all the answers.

Mark Lamberti

If I screw up, let me know

This is the success story of a man whose diary is planned three or four months in advance and, even though he has the driest sense of humour, candidly admits he might not be the most fun person to hang out with.

Mark Lamberti also believes the job of a real leader is to facilitate decision-making and not make a solo call. Having said that, he advises that you don't always need a 100 per cent information file to make a final choice. Prevarication can be a killer.

Mark is a Harvard University alumni, the founder of the massively successful Massmart Group and currently in charge of the Imperial Holdings conglomerate. His first job was selling furniture at the Bradlows chain for a salary of around R600 a month and that started a career in retail.

He believes in the value of time allocation, which he says is what you give to what you value most. It's that type of discipline that allowed him to oversee a business empire and also get his helicopter pilot's licence. He advises those seeking success to have some skin in the game as it focuses the mind. Mark says if he's got a big problem to deal with, he hits the hay at 8:30 pm and wakes up at 2:30 am to wrestle with it.

We meet in a booked-lined study or – as one who is striving to get one – the ultimate man cave. Mark says reading is a key building block to success, but with a caveat. "The last piece of fiction I read was in 1976, but I have never stopped reading. Fifty per cent of what I absorb is from newspapers and high-quality magazines and the rest is from books I can learn from – biographies, business books, books around the mind and how it works."

Some I have spoken to have either baulked at a definition of success or ducked the question. Mark was from an early age, as they say, a man with a plan.

"In my late thirties I crafted a mission statement which I carry everywhere with me to this day. A mission is not a set of goals. It's a statement of who you want to be. In the very first sentence I define success as exploring every dimension of my God-given potential. So I don't know whether I've been successful, because I'm still discovering parts of myself that are new to me. I'm always trying to do new things to discover new parts of me in whatever way, personally or professionally."

Most men in their thirties are either wondering what to do with their lives or are pre-occupied with a first mortgage and a young family. What, I ask, prompted the Lamberti document? "I think best in writing. Whenever I'm confused or having to think something through, I write because I think that that subjects one's thoughts to scrutiny by others, and it helps me to clarify my thinking. The specific thing that prompted it was Stephen Covey's book, *The 7 Habits of Highly Effective People*. He speaks about a mission beginning with the end in mind, and I did it at that time, and it's lived with me ever since."

Mark eschews the notion that one sign of accomplishment defines success. "I would rather talk about milestones, both personal and private, and the feedback I get from that. I've taken three companies public. I've celebrated my 39th wedding anniversary. I look at my children and feel very fortunate. So, the system gives you feedback and you must be sensitive to it."

In a high-profile and stellar business career there have been many hurdles and obstacles. How, I ask, does one pass or jump over them and not lose sight of the bigger goal. "You must understand context. I'm continually conscious of or trying to answer the question, 'Am I reading the context right?' I can piece together disparate pieces of data and see a picture. It's also easy to get derailed by the short term. With big decisions you need to think them through with a longer horizon. And the last thing is to mirror time. Reflecting on yourself, who and where you are and what your progress is."

Mark is a huge proponent of the power of the human mind and our conversation turns to thinking and how to do it most effectively. What's the secret? "The big questions need always to be on one's mind. You don't say, 'I'm now going to think for the next hour.' Big life and business issues need to percolate. I also have a mantra which is 'when in doubt do nothing'. I think that the passage of time gives clarity and leads you one way or the other."

So, how does it work then when a decision has to be made? Is there a process?

"You don't need a hundred per cent of the information to make a hundred per cent-confident decision. Sometimes with ten per cent of the information you can move. Other times you need to dig a little and say, 'Hang on, do I understand this properly? Are there other dimensions to this decision? Are there other consequences to this decision? Am I thinking about the second- and third-order effects, which is most often the case?' When you're running a business the size of the one I am, the last month or so can be determined by what we thought about strategically three or four years ago. My horizons are always far out and I have to ask myself 'what is going to change this business two, three, four or five years out?' As opposed to how we run tomorrow morning?"

That's a lot to digest. Feel free to pause and think. But not too much. We have work to do!

I suggest to Mark – fully expecting to be shown the door – that with this forensic approach to life he's probably not much fun to be around. And it's not a fun answer that he gives, which kind of proves my point.

"I think I used to be more fun in my younger years but people, generally, regard me as a serious person and I'm okay with that because that's who I am. I'll enjoy a joke and enjoy a social function as much as anyone else but I think if I get into a discussion with people, it gets serious and it gets philosophical quite quickly."

So, having established that he's not the guy who leads the Conga line at the Christmas party, let's move on to fear – both in life and in business.

"Nothing frightens me more than failing health. I've always felt the most valuable things in life can't be bought, and health is one of those. At this stage of my life you can only hope the energy levels hold. I sleep more than I used to when I was younger. I eat more carefully, exercise and I don't drink. I've got a collection of champagne upstairs that most people would be proud of and I think I've probably drunk more of the world's seven thousand different champagnes than most people have, but I don't drink at all now. I just find it takes the edge off."

While Mark says his diary is planned months in advance – it took us a while to pin him down for the interview – he says he *only* does the things that *only* he can do. The rest he delegates. That opens up a useful line of conversation, given that Mark says sometimes he delegates while knowing he could do a better job himself. The secret, he says, is in hiring. He tries to hire colleagues, as opposed to subordinates.

"I can say, hand on heart, that if I look around the table of my executive team, every single one of them is much better than me at something. I don't consider myself the chief decision-maker. I don't think that is what a CEO is. My job is to facilitate the highest quality decisions out of a group of people who are all functionally smart and share my vision. It's very seldom that I unilaterally make a call."

Reflecting on the values his parents taught him, the one word I seize on is frugality. Says Mark: "It's squeezing the last bit out of the toothpaste tube. Don't waste – and by not wasting it enables you to live a better life. Not miserly but being conscious."

And how then has that helped him in business? "Fundamentally, because the businesses I've run, most particularly Massmart, were high-volume/low-cost businesses and unless we ran them tight, they would never have been successful. That's why when you go into Makro you don't get plastic bags."

Given Mark's contribution to South African business, and his quiet philanthropy in educating scores of underprivileged children, he's allowed to dwell longer that most on the legacy question.

"I've often said what I'd like them to write on my tomb was, 'I told you I was sick' (see he can be funny). But I think the long term is created by what you do every day and I would hope my behaviour touches people in a way that leaves them slightly better off. Whether they remember me for it or not, is not important."

I'm going to take something from that last legacy line. Many of the interviews in this book have led to personal thought and introspection. And Mark's hope that he influences everyone he meets has resonance. I'm trying to inculcate that into my interactions now. With little success, I feel. But I'm new at it.

Takeaways

Successful people let big life and business
issues percolate.

Success means constantly reflecting on yourself
and what progress you've made.

Successful people only do the things only they
can do and delegate the rest.

Peter Vundla

No smarter than the other caddies

This is the success story of a modest man who, against overwhelming odds, changed the world of advertising in South Africa when the majority of the population were not deemed worthy or credible consumers.

Through sheer grit and determination, along with strong partners, Peter Vundla created the iconic Herdbuoys agency that took brands – some of them kicking and screaming – into a new age of business reality where companies were finally forced to see that the so-called 'township rand' had real impact.

Yet, when I sat down with him, his eyes twinkling, he immediately turned the tables on his inclusion in this project, suggesting there were others way ahead of him in the success queue. "I have always been in denial about being successful and won't ever call myself such. It is for others to call me successful."

Good start to the discussion, given we still have a camera rolling and thirty minutes of our appointment left. Come on Peter, throw me a success bone. A small one. Please.

He breathes deeply. Here it comes. "But if hypothetically I was going to call myself successful, I probably would define it as a considered estimation by others of my overall performance in life. I was always brought up to believe that one has to not only rise from the ranks, one has to rise along with the ranks. That, for me, is success. When I was growing up, success was defined in terms of being an adequate provider both to your family and in giving back to your community."

The old line goes, when you see a gap in the conversation, take it.

Peers, rivals and business partners all say Peter has been incalculably successful both financially and as a mentor and purveyor of wisdom. I'm determined to brush aside his opaque curtain of modesty. So, rising with the ranks, what does that mean?

"Apartheid allowed for certain people to succeed and to show that the system was not all bad. A few Black individuals who were successful at that time believed in that nonsense. But coming from a values-driven home we were told you know success on your own is meaningless unless you bring people along with you – your siblings and your neighbours. Whatever one did, you had to take them with you, because if you left them behind your success would be hollow."

Based on that definition of success, what are the values that drive it, and in your case do you still live with them?

"They're totally internalised and in my case integrity is at the centre of the wheel. If you've got integrity and you are going to work hard there is no doubt that you are going to operate excellently and achieve."

Peter says, central to his canvas of success are the relationships he has carefully constructed in his life. "If you have a relationship with your family, your neighbours, your tax man, your customers, your community, the world around you and the environment – and if your relationship is good with all of those people, then you'll live a whole, happy and successful life."

So if we've proven to some extent that Peter Vundla has achieved even a modicum of success, I have to ask then if it sits comfortably or with some difficulty. And his default humility re-emerges. "Some discomfort, I think, because I know I haven't achieved all of what I want to achieve and I know many around me have not done half the things I've done. How can I call myself successful when I play golf at the course I used to caddy at fifty years ago and I still find people there I carried clubs with? It makes me uncomfortable and in many ways angry because opportunities are still not given to all. Apartheid was about the denial of opportunities. Some of us got lucky breaks and it wasn't because we're any cleverer than the other guys in the caddy shack."

My one recurring question throughout this project has been about the lucky break. Peter says his was simply being born to the right parents. "My dad still remains my role model. He was an amazing man. My mom was a most gracious woman and they both taught me discipline, how to serve, about love, integrity and about speaking our minds."

Peter says his father came from a rural background and emphasised what he calls the dignity of labour, whether it meant cleaning a toilet or washing a car. Peter's life, though, was destined to be much more than manual labour, however poetically he describes the endeavour. And like so many other success stories there is, as he's mentioned, often the element of luck.

"I didn't have a mentor and I wasn't targeted to be a leader. I came from a family where money was not important and my father wasn't a businessman. By chance I got a scholarship to study business administration through an amazing South African called Fred van Wyk, who was the president of the Institute of Race Relations, and then a scholarship to study in New York where my interest in marketing and advertising started. I was also lucky to marry into a business family."

You can learn much about success from the people that other successful people admire. If nothing else, Peter's list is both extensive and eclectic, from the American financier JP Morgan to the actor Sidney Poitier. And there is a common thread, Peter believes, that binds them all together.

"None of them set off on their own. They were always assisted by others and they surrounded themselves with good people. I think all of them also had a fear of failure." And Peter readily admits that he's haunted by the same problem.

"I like people to look up to me so self-esteem is important. Without it I would live an unhappy life." Fair point. So how does one manage self-esteem? It's all in the head, according to Peter.

"I try to act like a winner. I'm always conscious about how I talk, what my thinking process is, how I dress and even the kind of car I drive. All of those little trappings of success help maintain one's self-esteem and, I hope, my success.

I want to go back to Peter's other observation of drawing in others who are as good as or better than you are. It's an important point and another common thread that seems to tie together all the people I've spoken to. Peter says it's about being sharp and observant.

"You look out for people you admire. When I went to boarding school I never mixed with my peers. All of my friends were older than me by as much as five years. I also made a conscious decision at a young age never to surround myself or associate with losers because I wasn't going to get anything out of them. I just don't want to ever be around negative people."

And he says meeting the right people is often about luck. Back to that word again. Let's give it another whirl around the block as it's a core pillar on which one man has built a life and a career. Peter says it's not only about recognising it but also about being able to ride it at the right time. On several occasions in his career, he says, he's been lucky to have been chosen for projects or partnerships over others with similar or much better qualities than his. If that happens to you, he says, and chances are it will, see the break that you've been given and simply run with it. Too many people spend time dwelling or ruminating about possibility, consequence, risk and doubt – and the opportunity passes them. He's not for one moment saying be foolish, but have the courage to seize the reins.

So, how much luck was involved in getting into the advertising game and eventually turning an entire industry on its head?

"When I got into the game during apartheid, the so-called 'Black consumer' – which I called the main consumer – was becoming more and more important. I was tipped off that South African Breweries had the Castle Milk Stout brand and its agency didn't understand the market that was consuming it. I did and I was chosen. It was a case of established agencies not understanding the main market and we rode on their failures because we were essentially talking to our mothers and our sisters."

During this conversation, Peter continues to point out that he does not consider himself successful. One chapter in his life that continues to haunt him is the infamous and well-documented Pamodzi affair. In his book *Doing Time* he says he agreed against his better judgement to become chairman of a company called Pamodzi Investment Holdings. He writes that he entered into a world of "intrigue, deceit, bad faith, abuse, poor governance and witchcraft".

Pamodzi would go on to invest in the catering, cleaning, security, tourism, information technology, healthcare, sports and entertainment, facilities management and financial services industries before going belly up. One of his mistakes, he concedes, was having little in common with those managing the business – and back, I suppose, to an earlier point about surrounding yourself with smart people.

Like many other successful people, Peter does reflect both regularly and meaningfully on legacy, but from a broader societal perspective. "One of the problems with Black Economic Empowerment is people wanting to cash-in quickly. It's not about living or creating a legacy. Right now for many it's just once-off short-termism. So the legacy I want to leave is wealth for my children so they can carry it through. I also want to be remembered as one who made a difference at the ad agency because when we started we really wanted to change the world and make it a better place. On my tombstone I want it written that I was a good man." Of that there is no doubt.

While Peter has had his detractors, there is no doubt that he has changed one specific sector in which he worked – and one that I am intimately acquainted with – advertising. Part of his bigger legacy is helping create a new generation of admen and -women who really understand the contemporary market – one which those before Peter and his merry band disgracefully ignored and disrespected.

As we pack up to go I ask him what the rest of his day is like. Will there be time for golf for the executive chairman of AMB Capital? Surely at the age of seventy he's earned nine lazy holes on a weekday morning.

"Young man, I might think about golf but I've also got to sit here and think about business. People don't do enough thinking." And therein is a useful parting shot. Successful people, it seems, are not afraid to sit and stare out the window every once in a while. Changing gears in this competitive world we live in allows time for reflection and it's often in that state the best ideas are fermented. I suspect, though, whatever is next, it certainly won't be an ad agency – a game Peter says is for much younger people.

Takeaways

Success on your own is meaningless unless you
bring others with you.

Success will be achieved if you have integrity
and a strong work ethic.

Successful people surround themselves with
good people.

Sizwe Nxasana

It started on a Putco bus

This is the success story of a man whose father instilled a sense of rightful purpose in his life when it came to the importance of a good education. Sizwe Nxasana heeded the advice. As a result he ended up running Telkom and the First Rand Group, sticking by a principle that a successful CEO should never be in the job for more than ten years.

He's now dedicating his life to improving the sad lot of schooling and tertiary education in South Africa through a successful initiative to build a network of private schools. He's also chairing the perpetually stretched and stressed National Student Financial Aid Scheme. Sizwe is living testimony to the oft-quoted Maggs Maxim that chartered accountants rule the word. He was one of the first ten black CAs in South Africa and the founding-partner of NkonkiSizweNtsaluba, the first black-owned national firm of accountants. He's also obsessed by fine automobiles. More on that later.

We embark on this discussion on a day when there have been more student protests, so education is a good place to start. "My father was a school teacher and I grew up in an environment where education was at the centre of everything my family did. I've seen how it has changed the lives of my family and the lives of people who were poor and under-privileged. Education opens your window to the world, exposes you to information, allows you and teaches you to think critically, how to analyse things and solve problems but also how to be disciplined and how to persevere."

And all of that, believes Sizwe, are the characteristics of professional success. Typical A-type personality, he's got the nub of the interview in the first sixty seconds and the coffee hasn't even arrived. So could he have scaled the heights of corporate success without the ethos of education that was so patently drummed into him by his father? His reply in the affirmative begins with being sent to boarding school in Lesotho.

"I started there when I was six years old and the experience taught me a number of things – resilience, an understanding of taking responsibility for my actions and being exposed to people who were really different."

Sizwe believes the attainment of excellence is an ongoing challenge and to that end says he's always taken himself out of his comfort zone in pursuit of new, unfamiliar and often frightening opportunities.

"I can never really call myself successful because there's always the next challenge. And I'm only as successful as my last achievement. Unless you continue learning and developing yourself you're going to stop growing and you're going to stop succeeding."

He advises people seeking success to embrace the tough ask. "I thrive best when I'm taking on challenges that are new and which I know little about. Sometimes you get frustrated and sometimes you get depressed, but it's how you psych yourself up to go back after failure. There's a lot more to be achieved and learnt from failure than there is to be learnt from success."

So the obvious question is, what is the secret to pushing through failure? Sizwe talks about digging deep and having an inner resilience but also the importance of having people around you who motivate and support you. He suggests you identify those people early on in your career and hang on to them for dear life. You'll never know when you need them.

I'm curious about this rather overtraded word in the success continuum called resilience. He might want to flesh that out a little, as we say in the interviewing trade. The first point is maintaining a positive state of mind, which I suppose is a given, but more interestingly, not surrounding yourself with negative people.

"If you try to surround yourself with people who think like you – who are positive in their orientation – you're more likely get a boost and that enables the toughness or resilience that you need."

All successful people, or at least the ones I've spoken to, set goals to a greater or lesser extent. But in Sizwe's case, it's about visualisation. "I always try to paint a picture of scenarios or settings that I would like to see myself in. For instance, when I started the audit firm I had a picture in my own mind and I visualised what this firm was going to be and what it would become. Part of it is that I grew up being told by my parents, particularly my mother, that I could do anything I wanted to." That, by the way, endorses the famous line by ultra-marathon champion Bruce Fordyce on his running genes and saying winning is helped by choosing your parents well."

Sizwe admits candidly that he remains deeply afraid of failure but he has a unique take on what failure is. It's another good life lesson for those of us trying to climb a little higher. "My definition of failure is when one doesn't try at all. But when you've done your best and things didn't work out, that's not necessarily failure."

Sizwe says success cannot be built on regret. Most successful people have an impossible work ethic and a gulag-like schedule. Sizwe is no exception. A workday typically starts at 3 am after just five hours of sleep. It's a gym session for an hour when he sweats, ups the heart rate and thinks about the day. But before any free-weights and the treadmill, he says he would have checked what happened overnight in the news; trawled through social media and checked emails so that when he's back from the workout he knows what the rest of the his day looks like. I agree it's positively exhausting.

I've also been curious in the success quest to ask people to define their personal brand. It's a useful recall meme if nothing else. Some have battled, others have pooh-poohed the notion. Sizwe is emphatic. "Humility with confidence."

Our conversation meanders back to people who have influenced him and he wants to talk about his mother. "I have six siblings. She made sure I went to good schools. She was a tough Zulu woman who taught us discipline but at the same time she let us loose. We had a particular routine that you had to be able take a bus and go to town to do something like collect the dry cleaning. I was eight years old when I made that trip into Durban. I took a Putco bus from Umlazi to Smith Street.

When I got off I didn't remember whether to turn left or right and ended up at the beach in exactly the opposite direction. It was getting dark, there were no cellphones then and I was terrified. When I got home it was dark and all my mother said was, 'You're back'. She was probably worried but all of us as siblings had to go through that ordeal. It was an initiation into how to count change, catch a bus and follow directions. That taught me how to navigate uncertain and unknown environments and knowing that if you believe in yourself, you may get lost along the way and even cry like I did the first time I went to town, but you'll be fine if you persevere."

It's a great life-lesson story, but all of that happened over fifty years ago. I suspect Sizwe might join me in suggesting you don't try it with your kids these days!

Sizwe worries that on his continuing journey to success he could articulate his feelings a little more – be a little more emotional – and less diplomatic. A quiet and measured approach, he says, can be misconstrued, particularly if you are angry.

Now let's talk about his love of fine automobiles. At any given time there has been a Rolls-Royce, a Maserati, an Aston Martin, a couple of Porsches and even a Bugatti Veyron in what I can only assume is a large and spotlessly clean garage. He believes cars can be works of art and concurs it's easier to fetch dry cleaning in one of those beasts than using a Putco bus.

While Sizwe was fairly emphatic with his brand description, he's iffier about the question on legacy. Does a man, I suggest, not get to a point in his life where he must start thinking about the footprint he leaves behind? "I think footprints are developed throughout your lifetime and I don't think there's a particular point where you suddenly switch on the legacy button. I think – unconsciously or consciously – based on what you do and how you conduct yourself, how you behave, how you treat others and how you relate to others, are all building blocks towards a legacy. It's about trying your best and attempting to help make a better life for others who may not have been as privileged as I was."

Takeaways

Successful people chase education because information teaches you to think critically.

Successful people believe there is more to learn from failure than success.

Success means painting a mental picture and visualising the end goal.

Nicky Newton-King

Don't fail the
five-finger test

*T*his is the success story of a person who says in over 7 000 working days at the same institution there are only around five where she would rather not have showed up. Nicky Newton-King is the powerhouse CEO of the Johannesburg Stock Exchange (JSE), who would like to spend more time on her bicycle and is hugely aware of the influence and responsibility that comes with being in charge of – as she delicately puts it – the centre of capitalism in South Africa.

Few would disagree that with the debate over inequality and monopoly, just warming up her professional life is a mixture of diplomacy and debate. Plus speaking for a constituency that, in spite of protestations of conscience and altruism, is driven by profit and high shareholder-expectation for their returns.

During our conversation from a top-floor boardroom with a telescopic view of the offices of several global banks, she takes issue with my observation that business in South Africa has been slow to take on government over issues of state capture and corruption. Nicky says most South Africans have no idea of the success and hard work involved in back-channel discussion. But more of that later.

I wonder firstly if she has a definition of what success is. Like others before her, we do the dance of whether she considers herself to be successful before we get the answer. It's fairly predictable. There are in my experience two types of successful people: those who shun the limelight and those who seek it; and I suppose in Donald Trump's case some who think they own and make the light.

Nicky says: "I'm not actually sure one ever reaches a clear point of success. I think there are different moments where you might be really exceptional and moments when you might not have hit the mark. I think success is a learning experience and a learning journey."

Okay a modest start – in golfing terms a safe first drive to the edge of the fairway. So is it something she's chased in her life, given that she's sitting on the ninth floor of the HQ of what can accurately be described as SA Inc.?

"Not the status, not the title, nor the chair I sit in. It's a privilege to be here. What matters is that what we do is not only of huge significance but also world class. So I hope it's the institution people respect and not necessarily me."

Nicky says it's not in her makeup to put herself in the front of a project or an operation but in the space of a leader that helps energise people towards an outcome.

Others I've sat down with have thought long and hard about the ego question. Nicky chips straight onto the green. And after this no more golf analogies. "I think you need to know as a leader that your energy, your vision and your ability to mobilise has a massive impact on your team and, to that extent, ego does matter."

But the clever caveat is that if you fail the famous five-finger test (What's In It For Me) you are bound to make the wrong decisions every time. Successful people seem to be good at mobilising others. Others might call it corralling or coercing.

What is the secret formula? Says Nicky: "Part of mobilising is speaking to the heart of people; to their passion. Because if you just talk dry numbers and you talk about where we're going from a financial perspective it will turn most people off. You've got to reach in and grab somebody's heart and soul to say that's why a particular issue or direction is important."

Our conversation turns towards super-investor Warren Buffett and a documentary on his extraordinary life in which he claims to eat a McDonald's breakfast every day and tap dances into the office. While Nicky might not arrive in her tap shoes, she appreciates the sentiment. "I think part of success is doing something that you really love. I wake up in the morning and I know what I am doing matters to the country. It is influence for a greater purpose. I would say to anyone chasing success you should get up in the morning and do something you're passionate about. If you're not, it's time to change horses."

Fair enough from the offices of the JSE but of course not everyone has that luxury. Fair point, she says, but being brave about career choices and not necessarily doing what your parents wanted you to do – or what society expected you to do – is a necessity.

Many successful people, in fact, acknowledge that most people don't end up doing what they really wanted to do in the idealistic teen phase of their lives. And that dictum applies to Nicky. She says at the age of four (talk about an early A-type personality) she wanted to follow in the footsteps of her father – a well-known lawyer. "I used to play under his boardroom table and knew I could be sitting at it one day. I pursued the dream, I have three law degrees, but then my father retired at the age of 35 and my mother became a professional farmer and that's the environment I grew up in. So, I have this deep legal training and am also a deep child of the soil. I love being on the farm and I still love the concept that women can do whatever they like."

But as chance had it, during her articles, the first person she worked for was the outside legal counsel for the stock exchange and, to cut a long story short, she never really left. So working in this environment where trading and deals are seen as a cut-and-thrust and no-quarter-given business, does a successful person need to be ruthless? Not at all, says Nicky. "There are moments when you have to make very hard calls and some people say the softest part of me is my teeth. I think I probably have a reputation for being hard when it matters and you should be able to have tough conversations, but they should end with mutual respect.

You can be ruthless; you can make the hard calls but you mustn't leave bodies in the wake."

I wonder then, in this high-octane environment, if she has any advice on how to make those tough calls. "That's experience. Judgement comes from making some wrong ones and also taking longer to make the right calls. There are going to be moments when others would have called it differently or better than you did. Good leaders should recognise that just because you happen to be the person in the hot seat it doesn't mean you have all the rights or all the wisdom."

While Nicky uses the word resilience when it comes to achieving and maintaining success, she also believes in the importance of cosmetics. And no we're not talking about a dash of mascara and a little lippy. The Americans call it optics. Says Nicky: "You cannot get into the basement; get out of your car and put on your grumpy face. If it's a bad day you suck it up and you walk in there with a big smile on your face and you walk slowly through it. It's not faking it because that belies the authenticity that you need to bring as a leader, but you do have to work through it. When it's tough the reality is you have to put one foot in front of the other and walk through it."

And by walking through it she means? "You confront the day and its challenges in bite sizes."

Leadership and achieving success is also lonely, says Nicky, but don't be afraid of it, she exhorts. "Don't sit at the office and have fear for the work space."

Another factor contributing to success, she believes, is having the right people around you. "Your biggest job as a leader is to find the right people, and preferably ones that don't look like you. People need to push you and if you want to keep a good team you must hire people who respect each other and who will be prepared to be a part of that cut and thrust."

So now we have the team in place all shouting to be heard and pushing her into a corner, how should a leader plan? Nicky seems to have that taped. "I wrestle my diary into what I think will be a useful allocation of my time three or four weeks in advance. I don't do lunches and I don't do breakfasts." It would seem her time is better spent absorbing and processing information.

Back to those smart people she surrounds herself with. "You've got to have people around you who are pinging you with new things. I'm naturally inquisitive and I've got a broad range of things I'm fascinated by. I'm a massive Twitter voyeur and I like to be challenged by an interesting thought. Youngsters keep you particularly grounded. The other part is to go out and find people who will challenge you. I love going to Davos (World Economic Forum) because it's like the cover of *TIME* magazine and walking with the people who are making the stories."

Nicky strongly believes that successful people have a responsibility to improve the lives of South Africans and that in her position as leader of, ostensibly, the centre of capitalism, that responsibility increases.

"We should be using *the exchange* in a manner that doesn't just work for the top one per cent, and the JSE should take the lead in having critical conversations about the huge inequality in society. Executives need to ask themselves how they can leave something that is better and more equitable than they themselves have. That's where I think I can use my energies to make a much bigger difference."

It's a fine and noble notion but in truth many JSE-listed companies pay lip service to that idea. How does this philosophy and ethos find real traction? Nicky replies: "Over time. But this conversation about conscious capitalism is a conversation that you're starting to see more and more in society and you will start to see more and more people being vocal about it. But you don't suddenly change something so deep-rooted by just saying 'well this is a good idea'. You actually have to say 'well let's start on the small things.'"

Unlike many other people I've spoken to, Nicky Newton-King has strong views on legacy. "From the day you start to lead you must start to think, how can I leave this place, this thing, this job, this role in better shape that I found it. That might not be personal legacy, but it'll help.

As a parting shot, and half knowing the answer, I ask her about her biggest mistake. And it's a well-documented story about a technology installation over-reach. Nicky cautions people not to be blinded by optimism. "There comes a time when you actually have to say this is not working or it's not sustainable. Success is the ability to make that call early enough."

One thing we didn't cover in our talk was gender leadership. Nicky is acknowledged as a pioneer glass-ceiling breaker. Hers is one of the few companies to have achieved 50/50 male-female parity. She says she doesn't define her journey in terms of gender and having to get over a hurdle. She says she knew she would be able to do whatever she wanted.

I hope the many talented women in the South African workplace are encouraged by that emphatic confidence and self-belief.

Takeaways

Successful people need to be energetic, which is key to mobilising a team.

Successful people speak to the heart of others – to their passion.

Success means having tough conversations but they must end in mutual respect.

Reuel Khoza

Practise positive dissatisfaction

*T*his is the success story of a venerable South African businessman who at times has been described as a pioneer, a thought leader, an academic, a trailblazer and – probably the one he is most proud of – a lyricist. That or the fact that he is quietly the country's second biggest exporter of avocado pears. Later we'll read the best way to enjoy them. For the record, a slice of crispy whole wheat toast, thickly spread with an over-abundance of ground salt and pepper is my preference, if you are at all interested.

Dr Reuel Khoza is not afraid to take on the establishment as he did some years ago as Nedbank chair when he raised the ire of the ANC by calling out what he termed a strange breed of leadership that needed to adhere to the institutions that underpinned democracy. The political climate at the time, he said, was not a picture of an accountable democracy. Some might ask what has changed. He went on to write that political leadership's moral quotient was degenerating and the country was fast losing the checks and balances that are necessary to prevent a recurrence of the past.

That was more than five years ago and he still stands by the dictum that all South Africans have a duty to build and develop the nation and to hold their leaders accountable. That underpins a philosophy of what he calls attuned leadership – in essence an insightful person who stresses the importance of human relationships, identifying with fellowship, winning trust and producing results in line with the needs of his followers.

We meet in a tiny boardroom where he tells me success is a configuration of a sense of accomplishment. It will, he says, vary from person to person. For some, it's material things, for others it's more multi-dimensional where you lift others at the same time that you rise.

And for him? "That I have done something positive for others and made a difference in their lives."

So what about the cars, the first-class travel and the recognition? The trappings that we all deep-down aspire to? "I see that as transient and, in the overall scheme of things, inconsequential. I believe you can only eat so much, you can only drive so many cars, you can only live in so many houses. I think what ultimately matters is your quality of life – a feeling of being intellectually accomplished and spiritually edified."

Moreover, says Reuel, it's having made a contribution in addressing some of the challenges that face society. That is a big ask for many of us who are looking to win, to achieve the kind of success he has. So against that backdrop, does he see himself as successful? And like so many others I've spoken to on this journey, his response is both humble and guarded. Sometimes I think I should have tried to speak to someone like Sir Mick Jagger who in the first 30 seconds of the interview would have told me how staggeringly successful he is and why. We didn't think he'd agree!

Reuel says success is all relative. "In the context of those that I grew up with – and here I mean in terms of material wealth – I'm relatively more successful than most. But more importantly, I see success in terms of what I set out to accomplish in my life."

He speaks fondly of his time at a mission school in Lesotho and a principal who he describes as balanced, moderate, sanguine, engaging and a person worthy of emulation. Reuel said the majority of his peers thought this man had attained what was not attainable. He (Reuel) thought differently and announced that when he was an adult, he too would become a principal. While it never came to pass, it does signify that Reuel was a goal setter from an early age and something he maintains is crucial in order to achieve success.

"I believe that without a goal you'll flounder. As an advisor to students later on in my life I coined the phrase: If you aim at nothing, you're sure to hit it, but if you aim high, chances are you will hit the target, overshoot it or fall just short, which will in fact be good enough."

But he says success is a lot more than a list of nice-to-haves or nice-to-be's. "It became progressively clear to me, even beyond setting a vision, one has got to have a sense of destiny and ask early on what your purpose in life is; what are you here for; what difference you are going to make once you have come and gone. That sense of future allows you to articulate your sense of destination, which many would describe as your vision, and all of those become clearer as you deal with life's issues."

So in a long and successful career, does he think that he's reached that destination and has he fulfilled that destiny? Firstly he says, people on the path to success mustn't become obsessed with or locked into goals because in life they keep revising themselves.

"I may not be a school principal but because of that redefinition and the receding of the goal I ended up being chancellor of two universities. I believe that's principalship. I also ended up being chairman of a number of companies. That is principalship as well."

Many successful people, it seems to me, know exactly the point at which they have made it. When they have planted the proverbial flag at the summit of whatever peak they are climbing. But Reuel cautions against over-optimism. Some might call it smugness. "I think once you feel satisfied, you cease to grow. A measure of satisfaction is acceptable but there should be no ultimate satisfaction for people who are ambitious. For people who mean to achieve, you need to have defining moments or stations in life where you feel you can look back and gain a sense of satisfaction. There is an African expression that behind every hillock there's another one and that should be the sense that urges you to accomplish even more."

So many of us will say once you've made it to the top of the hillock you're entitled to sit down and tell a few people about the journey. But in order to start on the next hillock – and I promise this is the last time I'll use the word – how do you push onwards and upwards? Reuel coins the phrase – a sense of positive dissatisfaction in which you simply have to tell yourself that there is more to be done.

"If you stagnate, you'll perish. So you must consistently push the envelope and push the horizon." Part of the process, he says, is starting fresh in order to prepare for the next onslaught. Reuel suggests that people should try to become less linear. "I'm a lot more diverse than being just a corporate or business person. I have an abiding interest in music and I have produced numerous choral music CDs. I have written lyrics for songs, I have written books. So I advise you to diversify."

He's also not the first person to tell me to stay in touch with young minds. "In a mentorship relationship there are times when the mentor becomes the protégé because in certain respects youngsters are more informed than you are and they positively embarrass you into acknowledging that you are not as knowledgeable as you fancy yourself to be."

I wonder if successful people have to be confident. And in his reply Reuel is emphatic. "I want to believe that without confidence you don't get anywhere, but it's more than that. It's also having high self-esteem and courage. If you are spineless, you're not likely to achieve much. I believe it was Churchill who said for those of us who would like to make a difference, for those of us who would like to provide leadership, the first, the synchronism, the prerequisite is courage, because without courage all of those kinds of things have no basis, the kinds of things that characterise one as a leader have no basis or foundation on which to build."

And he recited those lines ardently and without hesitation. So I guess having a memory for detail is also a pre-requisite for success.

Reuel rejects the notion of fear in the attainment of success but says something called "positive anxiety" is a given and should be embraced. He would have had a lot of it during what he terms his biggest failure, the 1986 project dubbed "Shareworld" – intended to be South Africa's own Disney World – that went belly-up. What then was the big lesson after that financial debacle? "In order for you to gain the requisite courage and to learn substantially, you need to try big and succeed big, if possible, but also be prepared to fail big. The important thing from failing big is to learn big. I learnt a number of lessons about business at the time; got to understand that unless there is a good balance between debt and equity or equity and debt, the chances are, and it doesn't matter how hard you work, the project will be fundamentally flawed."

Let's take a break here to talk food. Reuel is also a full-time farmer and a hugely successful avocado baron. My description, not his. So what is the best way then to eat an avocado? His face lights up. He clearly enjoys this subject and no doubt he will opine both creatively and seriously. Is there a secret additive? Is there a special way to cut them to maximise oil texture? Don't hold your breath. "It's a very versatile fruit. The best way is to eat naturally. You cut it in half and put in some Aromat." Really Reuel, Aromat? Jamie Oliver has nothing to worry about.

A question I've put to all the guests in this book is the one about legacy. Some have been too young, others take the self-effacing route. Reuel believes it's something you leave for others to define. "But I believe there are a number of things that should exercise your mind, even what you want to be remembered for. I want to be remembered for having lived my life optimally, having actively tried to love myself, so that leads to self-development, but also for loving my family. Here lived somebody who actually cared and – in large measure – also tried to share."

In closing our conversation, Reuel comes back to the notion of ethical leadership, saying anyone in a position of influence has a duty to stand up, stand out and shout out. This encompasses his philosophy of attuned leadership. "A leader who is not attuned to his or her followers soon becomes a leader in limbo and invariably then fails. Connectedness, compassion, empathy, integrity, humility, reasonableness and a determination to be effective are the keys to attuned leadership. An attuned leader can step boldly into an uncertain future with the certainty that followers will lend their support." Such wisdom – and the best he can come up with in the kitchen is Aromat!

Takeaways

Successful people value their quality of life and the feeling of being intellectually accomplished.

Successful people will flounder without clear goals.

Success is about becoming less linear and having many interests.

Imtiaz Sooliman

When you build goodwill the totally impossible becomes possible

This is the success story of a man whose life was laid out before him during a spiritual encounter in Turkey and for the past twenty years he has been at the forefront of disaster relief in places as far flung as Tibet and Haiti.

Dr Imtiaz Sooliman runs the massive NGO Gift of the Givers with military-like precision and for anyone in the logistics business it's a case study on its own. Apart from rushing to places devastated by natural disasters, his organisation also feeds thousands of destitute people in Johannesburg and our interview takes place next to a giant kitchen early in the morning, where massive pots of chicken stew and vegetables are being prepared.

And if that's not enough, he was an active, behind-the-scenes force in the 2017 release of South African hostage Stephen McGowan, held by the al-Qaeda organisation in Mali. He is driven by a perpetual internal energy and a deep relationship with God who, one suspects, has had a word or two in the past about him taking a proper holiday. He confesses that unless he has a cellphone perpetually in reach he is unable to relax.

Like so many others he too has an interesting take on success. "It's a state of contentment and inner well-being and where, most importantly, your heart and your mind are happy. In spiritual teaching we have a saying that if something disturbs you, your heart and your mind are wrong. But if they are settled, all is right." Not easy, of course, to find that inner contentment.

"It's an inner peace and you get it from your way of life. In my case it's about helping people. When I see the satisfaction in a mother whose child was hungry or people recover, or smile, or get a better quality of life, that is an achievement and the real meaning of success."

It's worth recapping Imtiaz's well-documented path not only to his success but how he started Gift of the Givers. It's a long story, so let me paraphrase. After qualifying as a medical doctor he was told about a spiritual leader in Istanbul. During an encounter at the height of the Gulf War, Imtiaz was acutely aware of a number of pilgrims of all races and creeds sitting and communing harmoniously. Later he was given an instruction by the teacher that most of us would baulk at and run a country mile. "He looked me straight in the eye and while I don't understand the Turkish language I understood every single word that he said. He said, 'My son, I'm not asking you, I'm instructing you to form an organisation. The name will be Gift of the Givers. You will serve all people of all races, of all religions, of all colours, of all classes, of any geographical location, and of any political affiliation but you will serve them unconditionally. You will not expect anything in return, not even a thank you. In fact, in what you're going to be doing you can expect to get a kick up your backside. If you don't get that then regard that as a bonus. You will serve people with love, mercy, kindness and compassion. Remember, the dignity of man is foremost. So, if somebody is down on the ground don't push him down. Pick him and lift him up. Feed the hungry, clothe the naked, provide water for the thirsty and even wipe the tear of a small child. Caress the head of an orphan and speak words of good counsel to the widow. Go back and this is now instruction for you for the rest of your life.'"

Success and deep faith are constructs that are often at odds with each other. You either opt for a life of sacrifice and humility or chase the money dragon. The two might be seen as incompatible. Not so with Imtiaz, who believes the very essence of success, both internally and externally, is about state of mind. "You have to be positive. We have a saying from the Prophet of Islam that whatever is going to strike you is never going to miss you and whatever is going to miss you is never going to strike you. If your intention is good, the door always opens up. I've had immeasurable challenges and my teams will tell you we have overcome them because of the right attitude. It's also about winning people over. Successful people need to remember they are dealing with people and not buildings."

Further, Imtiaz believes success is built perpetually on trust and goodwill. "When you build goodwill the totally impossible becomes possible. When we got to Nepal after the devastating earthquake some years ago we were told that, while authorities knew we were here to help, no non-Nepalese was allowed to work in a government hospital. We said we'll follow your rule but we also had a strategy. We had brought South African doctors who had previously lived in Nepal and we asked if we could, as a show of faith, help in one case. That led to a second and a third case and then we were asked if we could help train Nepalese doctors. Goodwill is built one case at a time."

So it would seem, after that story, that successful people need to be good talkers and schooled in the art of convincing. Imtiaz agrees. "You have to be honest about everything and to also be blunt. Say it like it is. I do that and they can decide whether they like me or not. In that way people respect you. As long as you don't insult them. When people know you're not messing them around, not patronising them and not doing it for yourself but rather for the benefit of other people, chances are your endeavour will be successful."

Part of that process would be the ability to win people over and Imtiaz says unsuccessful people fall into the trap of not respecting the belief system of others; or their attitude or their thinking.

Like so many others who have been successful, Imtiaz not only admits to making mistakes but embraces what he has learnt from them. It is, he says, not only having the courage to admit you're wrong but knowing at the get-go that you will be wrong. He says it took him many years to get not only to that point but also to one of collegiality. "In the beginning I stood alone and believed in myself. I didn't trust anybody. You've got to find people you can trust. I only realised that after fourteen years of running Gift of the Givers. It's not possible for an organisation to grow if a person holds back."

But like everything in life there is a balance. "You can't trust too much. Sometimes when you give too much leeway, people make silly and unnecessary mistakes, maybe because they are not as vested as you are so you have to reign them in."

I sense, though, the most important part of anyone's success is that thing called balance. "I think the biggest mistake I made was to neglect my family. If I were to live this thing again I would go back and try to control how I did it. I just went crazy. I've lost time with my wife and my children, and that's something I can't get back." His spiritual teacher – remember the sage in Istanbul who told him "I've given you something, you've got to use it" – also told him to have balance. "One third for yourself, one third for your family and one third for your work."

Given the darkness that he has encountered in his life it's a fair question to ask how he's remained positive. It cannot be easy seeing child victims of the civil war in Syria or abject human misery across hectares of a country devastated by an earthquake. I sense there is another story coming – and I'm correct. Says Imtiaz: "A priest in America had a physically and mentally challenged child and at a school function he, the priest, gets up and cries, 'Where is God almighty? Where is the justice of God almighty?' The crowd is stunned. They are expecting anger but the priest goes on to say he was walking past the baseball field and his son wanted to play but he couldn't even hold a bat. The kids on the field were hugely competitive. There were two more balls left to throw. If they put on the priest's son, they would lose, and if they put the other guy on, they would win. What will they do? They decide to put the disabled child on. And here is the miracle. All the players came from behind and held the bat and the ball is hit. They tell the child to run and suddenly the players from both teams run behind him and he wins the game for them. What does that tell you? The father says God's justice is in people's response as his son got positivity and hope because of the actions of ordinary children. They understood life better than most others."

The lesson here, he says, in all adversity, whether it be through tragedy, or even adversity at work, is that successful people are able to find that small sliver of light or, as some call it, the silver lining.

I can already see Imtiaz is itching to move on. He has people to feed and a planet to save, but I push for him to leave us with something big to chew on. I sense many more years and many more lives that will be changed or saved through the efforts of Imtiaz Sooliman and he's certainly not throwing in the towel. It would, after all, be a waste of a towel that could come in useful at another field hospital he'll build in another conflict zone.

He is thinking more of the next generation of South Africans, and at a recent graduation ceremony where he was given another honorary doctorate, he warned graduates not to forget where they came from and said they should not let their qualifications get in the way of their humanity.

Takeaways

Success is a state of contentment and inner well-being.

Successful people need to remember they are dealing with people and not buildings.

Successful people should find that small sliver of light or the silver lining.

Vinny Lingham

There really is a formula for success

This is the success story of a young visionary and a tech innovator who sometimes masquerades as a dragon and at other times as a shark.

While he might be famous for being a participant in two hit television shows that promote entrepreneurship, he is nothing like these menacing sharp-toothed creatures. He's a gentle soul who believes fervently in the principles of hard work; empowering others and a little down-time playing on-line chess. And coffee. A lot of it.

When I spoke to him in San Francisco, via Skype, he disappeared for an inordinately long time to find a cup. At one point I thought he'd popped out to a Starbucks – their headquarters in Seattle!

Vinny is the CEO and co-founder of Civic, an identity protection and management company. He was also the founder and CEO of the global search marketing firm incuBeta and its subsidiary Clicks2Customers. He is furthermore the founder and former CEO of Gyft and co-founder of Silicon Cape, an NGO that aims to turn the Mother City into a technology hub.

So was there a point in his life when he realised he had become really successful? I was hoping for a big Damascene moment, that row of red sevens on a noisy slot machine, a bolt of blue lightning, a large bearded man atop a mountain handing down a tablet. Not at all. His, rather, is a story of incremental progress, where the first chapter has already been forgotten.

"I grew up in East London and we didn't have a lot of wealthy people there relative to Johannesburg or Cape Town. So the perception of wealth and success is very different when you come from a small city. And so, when you have your first small business breakthrough I think that's when you get some sense of success and it gives you an inner confidence that you can achieve more than you think you are able to. The trouble comes when you have to maintain that trajectory."

Like all successful people it's also about the constant march of time and whether there is enough of it to achieve all he still wants to. And here comes a convoluted numerical explanation that only a tech-head could invent.

"I'm nearly forty now, so it's two-and-a-half per cent of my life. But when I was nine-years-old, one year was ten per cent of my life and that was four times more impactful for me. It's the same thing when it comes to wealth creation and wealth accumulation. The first million is the hardest; the second million is less hard. It's not a binary thing, it's more of a relative curve as you go through life."

WTF?

So for us mortals here's what I think is the translation. Time is always the enemy and success gets a little easier the more you keep at it. And by the way, I hate the word binary.

But while it might become a little easier, success accrual, to use Vinny's words, also gets a little more "bumpy" on the flight. So how then does he deal with the turbulence? Is there a secret to pushing through the bad times? What, Vinny Lingham, is the magic formula when things come apart and the wheels fall off?

He says: "I think the formula for everyone is different, depending on their skill and confidence level, but here's one thought. It does get a whole lot harder when you have more personal responsibility. If you want to be an entrepreneur, try it when you're in your twenties, try it before you have a family and life commitments. Give up that job prospect that's just going to get you a BMW straight after school. Give up that pursuit of instant short-term material wealth at a young age and pursue success in terms of your dreams. When you get a little older you need to have more reserves to weather the storms because entrepreneurship is not easy; it's full of thunder and lightning, especially when you're doing something different and you're challenging the status quo. Success means you're going to have to go against the grain. And going against the grain means friction, and friction costs money."

So, point taken, Vinny, you have to start young and the less encumbered you are the easier it might be. But let's tease that out a little. What distinguishes Vinny Lingham from other people who've also made a success of their lives?

There's a longish pause here and I'm glad we're Skyping on uncapped data. At least, I hope we are!

"Persistence is the number-one thing. As an entrepreneur, if you're not persistent you're not going to get through that stormy weather. If you expect it to be a walk in the park, then don't start a business.

"Then optimism. If you're not perpetually optimistic that you're going to succeed, you're not going to.

"And the third thing is insight – a mixture of your experience, your intelligence and the market opportunity you're seeing that no one else is – is why you believe in something that no one else believes in. And the reason it's so important is because that is your pure conviction for starting a company. If you can combine those together I think you'll be very successful."

Stop. Hold those horses. Lower the landing gear. So there is a simple formula, is there? Here it is:

P (Persistence) + O (Optimism) + I (Insight) = S (Success)

And to think I failed maths and now I'm imparting formulae in a book. My dead high-school teacher is turning in his grave. So now that we have the formula, how important is it for successful people to set goals?

Don't get obsessed, says Vinny. "Setting goals is tough and I've been bad at it for short-term objectives. I think it's more important to have a long-term trajectory that you apply in life. So ask yourself where do I want to be in five years, ten years, twenty? And then make decisions in the short term that align with that big thinking. Over a ten-, twenty-, thirty-year span in your career, as long as you're true to what you believe are your ultimate goals, you will be happy."

"But," says Vinny, "smiling when you can and having a lightness of spirit are far more important."

"You need to align your goals with what your goal for happiness is. If I meet a young kid who says 'I want to be a multi-millionaire' I ask them why. What would you do with the money?" And they inevitably say, 'I want to buy a sports car or a yacht'. And I say, then what? What are you going to do with them? What if you get bored with all that? So more importantly, people who want to be successful have to know what fundamentally drives them; what makes them excited; what makes them live; what makes them get up in the morning."

So, simply put, Vinny isn't saying money is not important in the pursuit of success. It is. Big time. But this next line is more important.

"Be at a point where you're just happy in your own skin and you're getting what you want out of life. If you make money the *only* goal, you will never achieve real true happiness."

Successful people, it seems, are meticulous planners and Vinny is no exception. His work day is driven by meetings and mails and then more meetings. But it's what happens in-between that is apparently more important.

"Don't ever forget to keep thinking. Between my routine tasks, I'm using the time to think about business."

And I think we might be on to something really important here. How, then, do you think about business?

Vinny says: "Successful entrepreneurs work simultaneously in the business and on the business and there's a time and a place for both. When you're a small team you're working in the business and you need to understand it, but you need to grow. That's why I tell people they have to have a co-founder, a partner, someone you can work with on building the business. When it gets bigger, you need to be thinking how do you upscale it; what are the marquee partnerships you can pursue; what are the deals you can make that will change the company?"

Vinny says in that respect he builds an ever-changing top-three to-do list.

"What are your top-three priorities for your company and yourself at any point in time? Should you have more on the list? Don't worry about them until one, two and three are dealt with."

It also seems successful people have a life built on varying degrees of fear. Vinny says he's perpetually scared of wasting his life. "I worked very hard as a young kid and I made a lot of sacrifices. They need to count now. They can't have been for nothing."

Successful people also seem to have a real handle on exactly where they are professionally positioned at any given time. Vinny, somewhat strangely, believes he's at the end of his career as an entrepreneur. Given he's not yet forty this is depressing news for those of us who might, or might not be, well over fifty.

Here's how he justifies it. "Technology belongs to young people with bright minds who aren't jaded by twenty years of struggle. They're free-thinkers. There comes a point when it's time to leave the stage."

But Vinny also believes those striving for success would do well to ingratiate themselves with younger people. "I only back people who I think are smart enough to see the world in the right way and for the time they are in it. In that way I learn all from them at the same time."

By definition, successful people are competitive. They always have one eye on the prize and the other on a rear-view mirror, looking anxiously at the opposition. In Vinny's case it's all about the team.

"If I'm working with the best people and if I'm networking with the best people, if I'm hanging out with the best people in an industry, I will continue to rise. Be among the cream of the crop. If you are going to sit and work in a dead-end company for five or ten years of your life, it's not going to take you anywhere. If you're not part of the progressive side of the economy, you are going to be held back."

Vinny says being competitive is also about future-proofing yourself. "You need to absorb as much risk as you can early in your life. So take the risk and work for start-ups as a young person. Take the risk and work for companies that are going to fail; that might fail; that could fail. And you know what, if you get just a little lucky you'll join a great company that takes off. And if you don't, you can move onto the next thing. But don't get stuck in a rut for a long period of time. And don't be a slave to a salary, because that's the biggest mistake you can make."

Successful people are also in conversation with themselves all the time and asking difficult questions.

"I have a company where my goal is to change the world and give everyone in the world a digital identification tool, whether it's on your phone or your computer. It is a very difficult concept. It's a tough thing to imagine walking through security at the airport and flashing your phone with an ID card that's digitally generated and making sure that it's actually perceived as real. It's very difficult for people to see a world like that. So when I wake up every day, the question I ask myself is, are we going to make it? Do we have enough money to make it? Do I need to raise more money? Do I need to change the strategy of the business? Do I need to find better clients or pursue different needs?"

So after that existential download, do successful people need any downtime? Netflix, Uber Eats and a lie down on the couch? In Vinny's case not so much.

"Sometimes I have an hour free and that's time where I can do research; where I can read something about my industry. But the reality is my life is a continuous seven-day-a-week cycle. So it's not as simple as shutting down on weekends. I'm always thinking about things. Essentially it's the notion that if work is life then you don't work. And that's kind of how it is right now. I also grew up playing chess, so if my brain's a bit fried and I want to just tune out, I go play online."

Success is also not for sissies. It's a hard-core pursuit of the impossible. Some years ago successful people started talking about their personal brand and specific attributes. Vinny does too.

"I see myself as a visionary, an innovator and someone with high integrity. I believe in integrity beyond reproach and hypocrisy annoys me."

Not bad brand architecture if you can get there. But if that's the pure marketing stuff, what about the esoteric, the spiritual? The God stuff? Do successful people need something bigger to lean on?

Strap in, this gets a little complicated. This is how Vinny sees it.

"I don't think, given the current set of circumstances in the world, it's easy to rule out the possibility of a higher power or to say it doesn't exist. But I think when you label yourself as belonging to one group or another you are forcing yourself to take on every belief in a specific system as opposed to picking and choosing. For me it's like a buffet versus an à la carte menu. It applies to religion, politics, everything. Free thinkers are people who say every fact is determined by the inputs you get. I'm born Hindu, but I don't practice Hinduism. I do believe in some parts but I also believe in parts of Islam and parts of Christianity."

Phew, who needs that Grande Starbucks now?

It's getting late in SA and the California business day is just starting for Vinny so a final question, the one all our participants get. Is he thinking of a legacy?

On the money side he's influenced by the no-favours Warren Buffett approach. "My kids aren't going to get my wealth. I'm going to teach them to make a living for themselves and live within their means. I don't believe in generational and legacy wealth. I take a lot of pride in making sure my kids are being raised well. My second goal is making sure they can follow in my footsteps in that I can inspire them to do things they want to do in their life."

And with a screen blip, the conversation is over.

Vinny Lingham is a new breed of South African cut from the same cloth as an Elon Musk to whom technology is a tool they have been given to help change the world.

Vinny wears his success comfortably, but he is acutely aware of the responsibility that comes with it. While successful people look for areas to exploit, they are also adroit at recognising others and drawing them into their personal orbit. It was said of former US President Bill Clinton that when he spoke to you, you felt you were the only person in the room for a brief moment. Vinny Lingham is the same. In his parting shot, he turned the tables, thanking me for inspiring him in his life's journey through my media career. I was flattered and, for just a moment, I was walking on the same lofty path he was on – and it felt good.

Successful people can, it seems, also draw others under their cloak of accomplishment.

Takeaways

Success means starting early before you have
a family and life commitments.

Success means being persistent.

Successful people need to be ever optimistic.

Bryan Habana

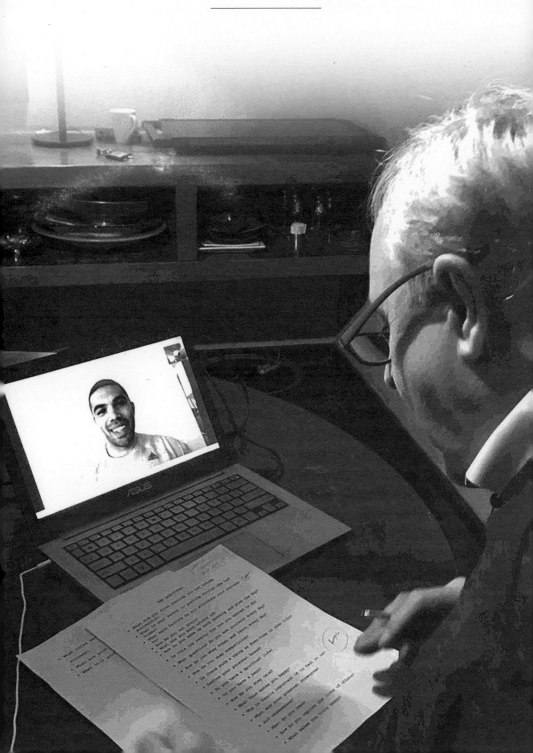

Show up, be present

T his is the success story of a sports star who, in a sea of a big names, has the ability to make a crowd of fifty thousand people or more draw breath every time he touches a ball because you instinctively know his tireless energy and brilliant unpredictability can turn a rugby game on its head in seconds. In a first-class career that has spanned more than a decade, Bryan Gary Habana has been a prolific try scorer – more than any other Springbok in history. It could be claimed his path to glory was pre-determined by his parents who named him after two Manchester United football legends, Bryan Robson and Gary Bailey, another successful South African.

If Bryan has one regret, even after reaching the pantheon of success, it is that he didn't complete his studies. In our Skype conversation from southern France, where he plies his magic, he dwells on that a lot, as well as the transitory nature of success and how important it is for successful people always to think of the next phase of their life – you must have a Plan B he tells me.

So many successful people can recount with absolute clarity the moment they achieved success, whether through a large amount of money in the bank account or maybe recognition through an award or peer accolade. For a star winger, Bryan's success was more like a lumbering prop forward. "My first-ever game of rugby was for the U14 G-side at King Edward School and wasn't quite the fairy tale start I had hoped for. It took me a long time to develop and it took me even longer to win a professional contract, having moved up through the ranks of the game very slowly."

During that time he encountered much hardship and adversity, but success started to come easier, he says, once he relaxed and started liking what he did. His sage advice is not to focus too much on acquiring success but to let it come to you. Part of that process, he says, as difficult as it might seem, is to not be overwhelmed by the huge expectation of success. Bryan also believes in self-reflection and reassessment. He says at every juncture of his career he's asked himself key questions about how he is performing, why he might be failing, where he wants to go professionally and, interestingly, whether what he is doing at any given point is what he really wants to do; and if it is making him happy.

You'd think that with all of that coursing around his head, he'd have little time to dart, weave, dummy and duck on the playing field. But it seems that rigorous and constant self-examination is key to his success. Part of the process is seeking help and he's not the first person to tell me that.

Bryan also suggests that success and failure need to be deconstructed and re-assembled from time to time. "Sometimes it's about going back to the basics and rediscovering what got you there in the first place." I'm intrigued by this exercise of re-assessment. It would seem to us mortals that have never had tens of thousands of people cheering you on and shouting your name, that sports success is the very definition of high self-esteem and a state of invincibility. Not at all.

Says Bryan: "The saying that the highest trees get the most wind is the absolute truth. It's at that stage of your career that you are likely to experience the most doubt and the most fear. At that point, as hard as it might be, you have to humble yourself and be open to criticism and when I say criticism I mean listening to people you can confide in and trust; people who don't really care about what you have achieved but care about you continuing to achieve something different. And it is scary. Most of us don't want to be told where we are going wrong."

I suppose it's easier not to get things wrong if there is a clear blueprint; a career map. Bryan agrees: "I was fortunate to be coached by Heyneke Meyer, who went on to be the most successful South African Super Rugby coach, and I will never forget him telling me ninety per cent of people that write down their goals become ten per cent of the richest people. I suppose if goals are just in your head you are dreaming about them and not doing anything tangible. I also think writing down goals becomes important when you are looking back to see what you have and haven't done."

So what has he written down in recent times, apart from having an injured knee fixed and starting on the path to rehabilitation? Most importantly it's that missing education component in his life. "I am starting to study again; something that rugby got in the way of and has caused me much disappointment in my life."

Bryan is one of many successful people who believe in the power of knowing people. So many people I've spoken to are inveterate business-card collectors and active on social media platforms like LinkedIn. It reminds me of a story my banker father told me about a senior colleague who was a favourite on the cocktail-party circuit. My father determined that his strategy was less about the two-olive Martini than it was about shaking the hand of every person in the room who could be of some use now or later in his career. The single drink was never touched and he slipped out without anyone noticing. He was lauded for his popularity and social stamina and this was back in the 1970s, long before technology made networking both scientific and tactical.

Let's get back to Bryan. "I'm focusing hard on making sure that the network that I have been able to create over the past fifteen years is solid and can open doors for me. Making the jump from sportsman to going into the real world is not going to be easy, but that is where planning is vital." And that might imply that for all the on-field courage, he is nervous about the future? Bryan concurs. "To make a complete life change after a number of years is a scary thought. I have been fortunate to have been very successful throughout my rugby career and hopefully with some good relationships that have been formed that will stand me in good stead long after rugby has finished. But that said, it does sometimes seem like a daunting task from having your flights and all the other logistics sorted, to now having to do all that stuff on your own. In my professional career most things have been done for me. Obviously it is not like that in the real world. But that said, I think I am really excited about what the business world has to offer."

Bryan is acutely aware of the responsibilities that come with success and says people who have made it or are on the path to success should heed them well.

"Successful people are people who can make a difference to those around them. Great leaders are people who make those around them spread their wings. Successful people are willing not only to give back but understand how hard they have to work to achieve success. Successful people are also willing to sacrifice. I have been fortunate throughout my rugby-playing career to have been part of amazing teams, with amazing captains, and that has rubbed off a little."

Given that there is an inextricable link these days between money and professional sport – some say too much is swishing around the system – how adept has Bryan been at managing his brand and what is the one word that describes it? I would have thought speed, excitement, courage, ability. Nope. It's humility.

"I am someone who has always given a hundred per cent but also understood how lucky I have been. Part of my makeup is not having an over-inflated ego and to be generous and well-meaning towards others."

It's clear from our trans-continental conversation that Bryan is very much a person who is acutely aware of his own success but more so of the community that has helped on his trophy-lined path.

Let me end with a quick story. I first encountered Bryan in a television studio where I was to interview him after another barnstorming performance. Television time is very much like inventory management. If the interview is at x-past the hour, that time allocation is about as set in stone as you can make it. I saw him arrive for the discussion and then there was an inexplicable delay and I was forced to park the discussion, move on and come back to it later. During a commercial break I went to find out what had happened to my star guest. And he'd been caught in the proverbial selfie and autograph cue among my colleagues. And not wishing to disappoint he'd simply remained outside smiling and signing. When I asked him about it, he replied with words to this effect: "You are only as successful as people will allow you to be. If you're dismissive they will dismiss you. Engaging with fans was more important that talking about myself."

I can see why the word humility underpins his personal brand architecture.

Takeaways

Success is achieved by not being overwhelmed by
the huge expectations.

Successful people always go back to basics and
rediscover what got them there in the first place.

Successful leaders help those around them spread
their wings.

Given Mkhari

I can't be when my people are not

This is the success story of a man whose abiding love of radio and desire to facilitate conversation among South Africans has created a fledgling media company that packs a punch way above its fighting weight.

Among numerous other business interests, Given Mkhari is the founder of the influential Johannesburg radio station Power 98.7 FM which has taken on the might of a bigger and better-resourced rival in the country's fiercest media market.

Given is an ardent believer that the more we talk, the more we'll overcome the myriad political, social and economic hurdles we face. I haven't told Given this before, but he used to annoy me when we first met. He was a young producer at the public broadcaster and I was working as an afternoon presenter on another radio station. As I left every evening he'd ambush me in the corridor and want to discuss minutiae of the business when all I wanted to do was get home and forget politics. I should have known then I was just one of many to whom he applied the sponge-technique – gathering up as much knowledge as he could from as many different people. Our acquaintance developed into a life-long friendship and I ended up working for him a year or so ago in what was one of the happier and more productive interludes in my professional life.

I learn quickly there are two sides to Given. Before our interview camera starts rolling he's full of bonhomie and jokes – and then he switches to a thoughtful and considered manner as the red light comes on. Before he even starts talking, I realise I've had my first lesson in the pursuit of success – be totally serious and focused when the occasion demands.

So how does he define success? "The ability to wake up every day and do what you choose to do but purely on your terms and at your own pace. But most importantly, do whatever you do for a bigger cause; and try to get paid for it." That's about as good an answer as I've got on this extraordinary journey. But I'm curious to know what he means by on his own terms.

"We all wake up and go to sleep alone in our own thoughts. If you have to live your life having to explain every move and every action, it can't be a meaningful life. Own terms suggests you have a true definition of what is worthy, what you value, your principles, your norms and your culture." Okay I think we're onto something here, but what about those days when that doesn't happen? When you can't motivate yourself to have that kind of enthusiasm and energy he talks about? How do you push through it? "Success has got nothing to do with enthusiasm. It's having a deep sense of conviction and pursuing a goal against all odds, even when it's not popular and when the world might not approve. It must all make emotional, spiritual, physical and, hopefully, material sense."

This is valuable stuff, so I let Given elaborate on this core definition of success and he tells me it's only come to him recently, through the success of his radio station (now stations). He says a critical component of success is conviction and purpose. "It is aligned to both desire and a feeling that I'm living the life I should be living; and also about honouring one's self and one's own unique personal architecture."

Let's pause for a moment and reflect on the difficulties of starting any business and notably a radio station and all its components, from regulatory and technical difficulties, to hiring talent and convincing advertisers to part with money on an untried and untested product. Overcoming multiple strands of adversity can't be easy. Given suggests it's about digging deep and examining or auditing your own character traits and isolating the ones that are most advantageous at the time. Using that approach in terms of leadership responsibility he says, "I am never at peace if my people are being led irresponsibly." And by "my people" Given's canvas is a little larger than yours or mine might be. With position, he says, a person has a responsibility to look out for others, whether they are friends of his children or people in his village back in Limpopo. "I have come to realise that no amount of money in my bank account is meaningful when, due to inaction, people are being compromised." That is a heavy responsibility for anyone to carry but Given believes his success was pre-ordained.

"I was assured at a very young age that monetary success was a given. It is in my name. My mother told me I was destined to succeed. So when that is obvious to you, even when things are tough, you can start worrying about other issues like what is next in my life; what is important to me and what is there to live for. What is my bigger purpose?"

So having parked the philosophical stuff for a moment, let's talk about money and risk. Given admits to loving chasing the deal and making money, but he's not obsessed with it. And in spite of his abundance of self-confidence, he cautions people on the path to success to be always wary. "I am a coward with conviction. I invest a lot of time in understanding something that I am going to enter into and how I could potentially mess it up. By the time I do it I am almost a hundred per cent convinced it is going to work."

Given's decision-making process is worth noting. He says most are made after midnight in the company of a cigarette or two, and once pointers are written down, it's critical they are soft-tested. He says he will seek the opinion of a variety of people who will either fine-tune his thinking, suggest he drop it, or tell him he is not thinking big enough. "These are not people that you necessarily agree with but you should have a high regard for their thought processes and experience. You must over-consult. The most irresponsible thing a person can do is not to tap into available insights and wisdom that are at your disposal. I think that is dumb."

All successful people screw up and the more successful they are the more mistakes they have made. The secret, says Given, is not only in developing a hardy carapace but in being kind to yourself. "Even if a decision bombs, and if the intention was right, I forgive myself quickly."

In another candid admission Given admits to suffering from anxiety but says the best way to deal with it is to acknowledge the condition and not fight it. He believes if you are in constant denial, you are in a constant struggle with yourself and that would be to the detriment of any successful venture. Perhaps of more importance than overcoming anxiety is not being afraid to speak out. Given believes that with success and leadership there is an increasing responsibility on a person to do what they think is right. "I am very vocal on political matters and the business, and I have been punished. You have to realise leadership is not a popularity contest."

Let's move on to the competitive nature of success. Given has two pieces of advice when one finds oneself on the losing side. First, he says, ask what part of yourself you underplayed rather than how the other person beat you – and then give credit where credit is due when you are beaten. Ask, he says, what the winner's unique approach was and what you can draw from their strength.

One person Given drew much strength from was his mother, who he says gave him an unhealthy amount of confidence. When he was two years old she was already telling him he might have a career as a Parliamentarian. And you should know that when Given was two, Parliament was an all-white abomination. She also taught him that leaders have to hold back. "If I am hungry and there is a plate of food, instinct says eat. But self-control, self-management and self-leadership means I need to pause and not think through my stomach but ask who else needs to eat; and then enable them to do so."

One thing we didn't touch on was the relationship between success and marketing, at which Given is a past master. Around the time of our conversation he'd hosted a controversial multi-media conversation with former president Thabo Mbeki and he had taken some stick for injecting himself too forcefully into the conversation at times. What his critics failed to recognise was that, apart from an informative and entertaining dialogue where we got to see a different side of Mbeki, the ratings for the event were massive and Given's name became a household one overnight. He maximised an opportunity and the leverage was invaluable.

Success in the hyper-accelerated world we live in is also about building, managing and sustaining a personal brand. Add an extra helping of self-confidence to the mix and the job is done. I suspect in Given's case, though, he's only halfway there.

Takeaways

Success means gathering up as much knowledge
as you can from different people.

Success is about pursuing a goal against all odds.

Successful people examine and audit their
character traits and isolate the ones that are
most advantageous.

Anant Singh

Get the team working

This is the success story of a man who lives in South Africa – Durban to be precise – but because of the nature of his business often works US (West Coast) hours. And not just him but his staff as well. So it's not unusual to see the lights burning in his office in the early hours of the morning. When Anant Singh was producing his 2013 magnum opus – the *Long Walk to Freedom* movie for which he had secured the rights due to a close relationship with Nelson Mandela – those lights burnt 24/7.

The movie was much more than a commercial venture for him, it was his personal gift and homage to a man he says was not only the essence of decency but the North Star that generations of future South Africans will set their moral compass to.

At the outset of this conversation let me declare an interest. I've known Anant for more than twenty years. We are not close friends. I have only visited his home once, where he makes an eye-watering prawn curry. He is, though, a clear-headed confidant and one of those people I would turn to in times of trouble. He also gave me my big television break when I hosted *Who Wants to be a Millionaire?* And when he visited the set, you knew it was business. He'd arrive with a set of notes and best you listened.

He is also a leading driver of the country's creative economy, having given many actors, producers and directors a massive break in the business. You also have to bring your A-game when you deal with him. Once I had stumbled my way through our discussion for this chapter, he turned the tables on me and starting quizzing me about winning and success. I made no sense, of course.

While he believes his career has been successful, he adds that the movie business is littered with failures, of which he's had his fair share. Those failures, he says, are an important component of success and people striving for excellence need to understand that they are a vital part of the journey.

There is an old cliché that usually applies to sportspeople who are sometimes given what commentators call instant status. The line goes, if I recall correctly, that it's actually taken them twenty-five years to achieve overnight success. In Anant's case that is absolutely true. It took him more than twenty-five years to finally realise his dream of putting Mandela's story on the silver screen.

"That comes as close to anything for me as pure success," he tells me. Long before he (Madiba) was released I was writing to him in prison to seek his permission. The one thing I remember was his modesty and asking me long before granting the rights why anyone would want to watch a movie about his life. It took a long time to make but in film terms it was about as good as it got. That is probably my crowning moment of success."

Given the close relationship that Anant shared with Mandela it would be foolish not to explore his understanding of this giant of a man and what made him the epitome of success for so many people. Says Anant: "I don't think he ever dwelt on the issue of success, what it meant and whether he thought about it. For him – and this is a hallmark of really successful people – it was his ability to really care deeply about people first and then issues. And it was never lip service, he had remarkable empathy. I considered this a remarkable talent and strength. I'd be in New York with him and we would walk through the kitchen and he'd talk comfortably to staff; and then, just moments later, would be a commanding presence with kings and queens."

Anant believes Mandela also had a genuine authenticity, whereas lesser people when given a stage or a pulpit often use it as an opportunity for personal gain. So what might the pupil have learnt from the teacher? "Humility, leadership, a sense of values – all the things that we are lacking in our country today."

Anant says Mandela's other success secret might have been the ability to make a difficult decision and then follow it through to its conclusion, in spite of obstacles in its way. So is an assertive nature a prerequisite to success?

Like others between these pages, Anant says he was a lot more difficult and demanding in his younger days but with the passage of time, greater experience and more maturity, he's dialled it back somewhat. But he says being assertive or forthright also depends on the task at hand. For instance, when you're producing a film with thousands of people involved and many millions at stake, you have no choice but to be assertive. Anant says the skill is knowing when to use it and when to take a softer line.

So many of us operate on success in the past and obsess about attainment in the future. It might be better for many of us to live in the here and now.

Anant has never been a goal setter or a dream chaser. "I've always operated in the present. I deal with what I have to deal with in the moment. There's no master plan. I just follow my instinct."

It's that last descriptor that I think we need to tease out.

"In the movie business there is no formula. Every day you must expect to be surprised."

He cites this example when the word unexpected won the day. One was a movie in Zulu about South Africa's AIDS crisis. He says it was never intended to be a success, but it was the first South African film to be nominated for an Academy Award. The lesson here is a good one. Don't overthink things.

Our conversation turns back to success and failure and Anant believes failure is indispensable to achieving better things later in life. "You have to fail and you must embrace it, learn from it and move on." The secret here is not to dwell on failure just as much as not dwelling on success. It's back to that living-in-the-moment thing, I suppose.

He adds, though, that while you shouldn't spend too much time on fruitless introspection, failure should teach the harsh lessons in life. "When I was starting out I sold a business and either friends or family wanted to borrow some money, and I lent it to them. I never got paid back but that was it, no more lending money ever. Nowadays, if somebody wants money and it makes sense to me I give it to them."

So many South Africans think that the proverbial grass is always lusher and a shade brighter in other places. Anant believes we overlook the huge potential South Africa still has in spite of this rollercoaster called uncertainty and hardship that many of us are riding. Here's his take and it's about the advantage of relative solitude and distance in a crazy world: "Being in South Africa, you can separate yourself from the craziness of what is in the US or in London and make decisions more rationally. Let's not also forget we have great creative and technical talent."

Anant says his greatest weakness is an inability to listen carefully. He says it seems to him that many others who have scaled great heights have a rare ability to take soundings from a variety of people and craft the best solution from the collective input. He says he's still learning that skill. "I'll take opinions and then say 'to hell with it, I'm going to do it my way'. It's worked sometimes, other times not."

If that is his approach, then, is he a rule breaker? Anant changes tack and replaces the word rule with accepted guidelines, which he says don't always need to be broken but may need to be changed. This man should go into politics with spin like that.

It was at that point that he turned the tables on me and started quizzing me about my life, my accomplishments and my views on winning and the attainment of success. As much as he batted some of my questions away with deft subject changes, shoulder shrugs and head shakes, I found myself doing the same. I asked him why. Some successful people love talking about themselves, he said, and others, even though the light finds them, are happier, not necessarily in the shadows, but on the periphery where it's safer and quieter and you can get on with things.

I walked away from the discussion having learnt a little more about myself, which I suppose was going to be an inevitable part of this journey.

Takeaways

Successful people see failure as an important component of striving for excellence.

Successful people have the ability to make a difficult decision and follow it through in spite of obstacles.

Success is not necessarily breaking the rules but sometimes altering the guidelines.

Gideon Galloway

Live life at
1.5 x normal speed

This is the success story of a man who believes emphatically that because of the time we spend at work we need to maximise the fun factor and who has put his spiritual beliefs at the core of his business.

Gideon Galloway is the founder of the King Price Insurance company, which has built a reputation for disruption in what is often a staid and, let's be honest, boring industry. Walk into his Pretoria head office and you could be forgiven for thinking that the company has modelled itself on a circus. Bright colours, an indoor call-centre roller-skate track, an overabundance of toys and gaudy ornaments on display. Then add to these an exuberance from staff that has to be genuine because no one could imbibe the amount of sugared energy drinks it would take to achieve that state of mind.

Of more importance, the company has two staff policies that beggar belief. When you join – so confident is the company of its hiring practice – if, after a month, you find the culture is not to your liking,

King Price will pay you thirty thousand rand to leave. The argument goes that it's more expensive to change the attitude and persona of an unhappy member of staff than it is to pay them to hoof it. In five or so years only one person has taken advantage of the offer. Senior staff are also given unlimited leave, providing they get their work done. So, Monday hangover? Cue the morning in bed without anyone phoning up and yelling at you. The thinking here is that human beings are primed to be productive. We want to work.

After the obligatory walk-through where I could have sworn I saw a clown lurking in the shadows – but it could have been the coffee – we get down to business. Gideon says he wasn't wedded to building an insurance company when he started but wanted to create something that would make a difference to peoples' lives, had its own unique culture of caring (and hilarity) and also had long-term franchise potential. You have to admit franchising an insurance brand is innovative. I didn't ask him if it perhaps had drive-through potential. "I'll have two car policies, yes supersize them with a side-order of fries." You see, the fun at King Price is annoyingly infectious.

Let's start with this culture thing. Gideon believes the more enjoyment people get out of work, the more productive they are likely to be and the company's results will be concomitantly better. So, what informs and drives the culture that enables your success and has caused rivals in the sector to smack you over the head with your sceptre?

"I think you can see the energy and friendliness. It's not the toys and not the interior design but the ambience. It's about continually energising people and energetic people are more successful. I learnt early in my life you can't make a person do anything. They must want to give you their time, their passion and their heart and if you can get that right – one passionate person is worth three others who are semi-engaged."

But to maintain the culture, to spin the flywheel of success can't be easy – or is it? "Design, it seems, does have something to do with it and I'm a person who abhors the open-plan-office concept. It started off in my previous company where I knocked all the offices flat," he tells me. "I was then asked if we wanted noise boards for the call centre. Suddenly there was this buzz. People felt more approachable." But surely it's not just about taking partitions down? "I do think it starts from the top. It's the friendliness. It's how leaders treat people. It's being humble and not arrogant."

Now we're getting somewhere. A different take on success. What did he mean by being a rebel where in a business as precise as insurance there's no room for that type of approach? Right back at you from Gideon. "No! Breaking rules is how you get ahead. Yes, we are regulated as an industry but successful people can still tick the right boxes by challenging the status quo. In the end we said, who said financial services can't be fun?"

So how did he break from convention? On the cheap, it seems. "When we launched we had five guys from varsity that could donate their time and experience, and who believed in our goal and vision. All of the staff that joined from the start took salary cuts. Even after we launched, our advertising caused a stir in the industry by using the words 'super cheap'. Ad agencies told us never to use the word cheap as it suggested the product was inferior and could not be trusted. Yet, I would take two placards that said 'low-low premiums' or 'super-cheap premiums' and I would walk around the office. People are just too scared to try new things."

And that is another pearl to add to the success primer. "A little bravery never hurt anyone," Gideon cautions, but that with time, success and scale – breaking the rules does become a little more difficult – but you have to hold on to that ethos. And scale, by the way, is another of his real goals.

"I think when you become bigger things become more regulated. At one point you had nothing to lose, then you have clients. But we say to ourselves, 'never become a corporate giant', and every now and then we take a refresher, a strategic breakaway, to counter that."

So far it all seems to be working. Our conversation dips briefly into the genesis of the business and the lessons to be learnt there. He grew up in Nelspruit, studied computer science for a while and then, before he graduated, discovered beer. "At twenty-three I was asked for a third time to leave varsity and my dad said this is it; enough is enough."

His father's business had just been liquidated and Gideon ended up being a waiter at a church camp. One thing led to another and in a journey that cemented his religious beliefs, he also started website design and ended up being one of the driving forces behind the insurance quote-comparison site Hippo. That eventually led to the formation of King Price, which it's worth noting, is built on a principle of institutionalised altruism and of giving a large percentage of profit to community-outreach projects.

So, firmly established on the insurance throne, how driven is he? When he wakes up does the ambition kick in immediately? "I'm still very hungry but more controlled now. In the past, I was a workaholic and it wasn't healthy. I never stopped. I would drive, listening to business books and do anything to get more knowledge."

While having a family might have slowed him from 6th to 5th gear he still lives by the dictum that every day that he does nothing is a huge opportunity missed. And to that end he is modest about his accomplishments and does not believe that he is even close to achieving what he is capable of. But he does recall with great clarity the first sip from that sweet cup of success.

"Soon after our launch and not too long after we started flighting TV commercials, I was standing in the call centre, willing the phones to ring and they did. I sat still and listened and it was the first time I relaxed, let it sink in and said to myself, 'Wow, we did this.'"

Here's another piece of advice from Gideon: when you start achieving a degree of success, however small, stop, pause and savour it because the moment passes quickly as the new hill looms large.

And now the conversation starts to pick up as we hit the success-vision matrix. Says Gideon: "If I see it in my head, I already believe it and then it's just about getting the right people involved." But watch out for the big mountains, he says, because they will always be there. "Nothing is ever like a spreadsheet but obstacles should never change the vision."

But success, he says, is also built on flexibility. "I don't believe in strategy think tanks because in today's world everything moves too fast and you have to adapt quickly." If you don't, says Gideon, you'll die. We get the picture.

He also exhorts those on the bottom rung of the success ladder to practice what he terms seagull moments. For those not schooled in business ornithology it involves dropping something from the sky. Go figure. "It's when I send an email out of the blue. If I haven't spoken to someone for a while I ask what's happening in their life." Gideon believes that ad-hoc contact creates a cohesive and winning culture.

Gideon believes that a default position that many executives erroneously adopt is to attach themselves professionally to an older person. Change the paradigm, he says. "It's only recently, and for the first time, I've had somebody younger than me in a quasi-mentor type of role." You'll be surprised what you can learn, he says.

I wonder whether Gideon's relationship with his father might be a complex one. It often is for children who are more successful than their parents, even though it's what they all hope for. Gideon says a key moment in his life was when his father said he was proud of him. "We grew up getting compliments but in the wrong way, almost like in the army or boarding school. After that church camp I wrote down all my issues in life and wrote my dad a letter saying I was sorry for not getting my degree but I now need to carry on. It's only recently he's shared that he's really proud of me."

While earlier Gideon was preaching an anti-spreadsheet gospel, he concedes that he has worked his life out on such a document. Everything from how he'd like his children to grow up, to the big plan of having King Price operate in over thirty countries in the next decade. And the 'shortish-term' plan (2027) is for a digital bank.

Takeaways

Successful people enjoy their work and
consequently are more productive.

Successful people see every day as one filled
with opportunity.

Success also means pausing and savouring it
because the new hill to climb looms quickly.

Ryan Bacher

Solve a pain point with same-day flowers

This is the story of a man whose path to success has been paved with vases of flowers, fancy chocolates and even the odd balloon. Ryan Bacher, a member of an iconic South African family that has cricket surging through its DNA, is the founder and face of the hugely successful NetFlorist. This is the online gifting service that at times, like Valentine's Day and Mother's Day, measures incoming orders by the second. A career highlight is being at the nexus of a long-distance cyber transaction between one of the most famous men in the world and one of the richest (more on this shortly).

Ryan's cramped Johannesburg office sits atop a sprawling process warehouse where arrangements of flowers are assembled and dispatched from the early hours of the morning in a fleet of pink trucks daubed with cheeky slogans.

Like many entrepreneurs more concerned about daily output and workflow than fancy trappings and niceties, he offers a mug of instant freeze-dried coffee and is far more comfortable talking about the business than himself.

"Before we were around people phoned a florist they didn't know and asked what the beneficiary would be getting. Often the experience was unsatisfying and people could feel cheated. And then suddenly you could go online, you could have a look at what was on offer, and get it delivered the same day. Then we realised after a few tough years that this thing was really valuable to consumers and if it's valuable to consumers we could build a real business out of it."

And that might be success lesson number one from Ryan Bacher: seeing with absolute clarity bigger potential through daily hardship and adversity. But, come on, Ryan, this isn't a story just about your business, it's about the person who built it, who put in the hours, who tasted the bitterness of failure. Again he prevaricates on the definition of personal success. But it's a clear indication that many successful people don't see too much distinction between their own lives and that of their business or project.

Says Bacher when pushed a little: "I think it's probably defined by offering value to customers, staff and shareholders. If our staff is getting value, be it growth as people or fulfilment in the workspace, and most importantly our customers see the service that we are offering is valuable to them, then I think that's personal success."

But here's a little nugget. Success is not all about the moolah, the Maserati and the Mont Blanc. "I genuinely don't think it's a money thing. We could be making a little money or a lot of money, but if we tick the other boxes I've mentioned then I think it's some measure of success."

One of the hidden mysteries in determining a success matrix is how important it is to an individual and if and when they started chasing it. And in true Bacher-family style, with a few cautious runs on the board, he can afford to go for a big hit. "I definitely think I'm driven a little too much by ego and the need for NetFlorist to be a good story – and how it makes me feel. There's definitely a connection there with success but I wish there wasn't. I wish I could detach my ego from it, but I don't think I can," Ryan says.

So are we on to something here, how much ego is necessary in order to be successful? On the ebullience and self-esteem-metre, does the needle have to stay in the red? My hope is that it does – all the time. But Ryan is having none of it. In cricket terms he plays a forward defensive shot to a tricky ball. "I'm not actually sure if ego will help you get up in the morning and do big things. I wish I didn't have it."

So while ego might play some role in his success, peer and market perception is more critical to Ryan. "I wish I was doing it just because I wanted to do the best I could, rather than for how other people perceive the business to be. But I am who I am and I would love to disconnect more."

That's another concurrent thread that runs through the lives of successful people, a perpetual desire to step back sometimes, take a breath and disengage from the complexities of their lives. But they seldom do and the lesson is to accept the burden of leadership, however onerous and energy-sapping it is.

So if that is to be believed, what then is the secret to pushing through those tough times? In Ryan's case it hasn't always been a bed of roses. He ignores the pun. I sense he's heard it many times before. It does, he suggests, come down to two simple things: an abiding self-belief – a difficult coat to wear – and a perpetual fear of disappointing one's customers. We've heard that one before. "You have to create value for consumers. If you're not giving them something that is intrinsically valuable then I don't know if you have an idea of business or success."

So what happens when the solution isn't easy to find? Successful people, it seems, know when to stop and call it a day. Throw in the towel. Run up the white flag and say they are proud to have tried something and failed. "We've done that many times in this business. Some years ago, we had this grandiose idea to open retail stores. We thought, how hard can it be? So in true entrepreneurial style instead of building one and seeing how it went, we decided to build several at the same time and after a year we realised we didn't have a clue how to do it. It cost us a huge amount. It was a terrible mistake. And worse, it took our focus away from the business."

So, failure aside, which all successful people say is not only a badge of honour but a must-have, how much structure is needed in one's life to constantly be playing in the Premiership or the Majors, as the say in the US? For instance, is goal-setting important to success? His answer is unsurprising. Unlike many of us ordinary folk, Ryan sits down every year and commits something to paper. He says it's useful to have a benchmark, something to measure, something to aim for. "I don't know if these goals have much to do with success but I do set them, particularly in my personal life, and probably hit half of them."

It's all pretty stock-standard stuff, family time, gym, eating properly, but it indicates three things: the importance of a work-life balance; the ability to compartmentalise and the notion of a life structure, but over a period of time that too might change.

While successful people often appear to be invincible, bulletproof and indestructible, a certain amount of fear is always evident. Ryan is not ashamed to admit to a little terror at times. "My biggest fear is that my business doesn't continue to be successful and grow. I've put so much energy and time into this. It is my life. I'm not sure I would want to walk away."

In Ryan's case his fear interestingly manifests itself in being risk averse, which, of course, would appear to be the antithesis of entrepreneurship. "I'm a weakness in my own business, I think. I'm probably too conservative and I think that might be attached to the fear. But it's a balance. It's sometimes a fine line between betting the farm versus I don't want to lose this precious thing that I built."

So while big goal-setting is important, how critical is planning the minutiae in the pursuit of success? That old attention-to-detail thing. Coping with the daily grind. Knowing which meeting to attend, who to call and which report to glaze over. So how does Ryan Bacher start his day? For those of us who have perfected the art of perpetual procrastination, this is a small slap across the face. "I try when I get in every morning – and in the first half hour – to attend to the stuff I really don't want to do. It's easy to come into work and do nice things but there's always hard stuff to accomplish. It's a process to go through but this is my business and my baby. When customers are angry it hurts me and so it should."

Most successful people are worriers and question where they are, where they are going and if what they are doing is really what they want to do. A little existential but true nonetheless. It's a constant battle of the inner soul. Let's return to our cricket analogy. While Ryan has been adding runs to our conversation scoreboard, this ball troubles him as I ask him what he really wanted to do with his life. "In this business or in general?" "General." "In general?" "Long before there was even the speck of an idea of NetFlorist."

Ryan takes his time answering, despite having a business to run, anniversaries to acknowledge, guilty husbands to help and I think I might have forgotten to order flowers for someone … "I have a weird history. I went to university, I did a law degree but I played tennis my whole life and started coaching when I was at law school, which helped pay the bills. I would say that I'm more of a natural teacher than I am a business manager. So I think I probably wanted to teach. I think I am better skilled for that, than this thing. I think I'm only average at this, if I'm truly honest." So finally a chink in the armour, a ball that almost nicks the stumps. While self-belief is critical, Ryan, like so many other successful people, also concedes to some insecurity and doubt. Good for him. Too much chutzpah can destroy both the man and the myth.

Now it's time to go in for the kill. Here comes the big question. "I wonder then, Ryan, if average, which is what you've just described yourself as, makes you more competitive? In other words, do you have to try harder, compensate, mask the low self-esteem because you have that doubt that sometimes gnaws at you?" And with a deep breath here comes the admission.

"No question about it. I have a fear all the time about this business not succeeding. I'm not sure I have the confidence. I have friends who are entrepreneurs who genuinely believe that if whatever they are doing today doesn't work, they'll just do something different tomorrow and it will be better. I'm not sure I have that level of self-confidence."

In my business of interviewing, once the big fish lands, in this case fear and lack of confidence, we usually gear back and ask something easier like, what did tennis teach you about business?

"I was comfortable to lose the first set and had some self-belief that I would still be able to win the match, so I would play people who would head out the gates early, but then I would catch them at the end. So if I applied my mind in a business sense, even if we had early setbacks, I knew we would be able to get around it, but with a huge amount of luck. I cannot tell you how much luck and timing has been involved in this business." Luck is a key ingredient in success. Ask anyone from Moses to Madiba. "And," Ryan says, "it's what you do with it.

"I think you've got to see it, acknowledge it and take advantage of it. I picked flowers for no particular reason. If we hadn't done that – if we'd, say, picked couches – who knows what would have happened. So, you can only put that down to luck. Yes, we took advantage of it, but it's luck; then we put in our effort."

So the man wants to talk about his flowers, bearing in mind he knew nothing about them before he started the business. Let's do it, as I ask him to look over his left shoulder at a vase of roses and ask what he really sees. Is it a unit of delivery? A micro line item on a profit and loss account? A living symbol of happiness? Boy I'm on a roll here. People who are successful in business often have an ability to see how their life, their contribution, their product or their service goes way beyond the obvious. Even a bunch of flowers. With a ribbon.

Says Ryan: "That thing is utterly meaningless without a message. So when people ask me what it is I do, I say we deliver messages. They might say 'I love you' or 'I'm sorry' or 'Get well'. But that message on the card is actually what we deliver. The flowers are just the process by which it comes packaged."

Successful people seem to see a higher purpose in their life. I once interviewed the MD of a hot water geyser factory who believed he was improving the nation's collective psyche because mood was improved after a hot bath. For the record, Ryan uses his own service a couple of times a week. I didn't ask if he gets a discount!

Successful people, it seems, while having a greater purpose, are also multi-layered in their emotions. While you have to be tough to get to the top, compassion, empathy and the EQ factor – are also important. And here comes one of my favourite stories from this entire success quest project prompted by this question. "I'm sensing there's a soft heart and you must look at some of those messages, are there any that resonate with you, that have touched your life?"

He replies with the story I hinted at near the beginning of this chapter: "In the early days, I used to look at all of them. Later we won a tender when Madiba (Nelson Mandela) was ill. At one point somebody in my call centre phoned me and showed me this message: 'We're thinking of you, we hope you get well soon – Bill and Melinda Gates'. That was pretty cool because for one transaction to touch two of possibly the most powerful people in the world – certainly the most recognisable – was astonishing." Of course, I had to ask how much the billionaire spent on the arrangement but Ryan moves the narrative quickly on to Valentine's Day and the notion of work ethic. I don't press him on the Gates invoice. I'm on his database and would hate in future for a birthday bunch of roses to be mixed up with Mountain Laurel, Ragwort or Veratrum – if you don't know, three of the world's most poison-filled flowers.

It's time to start ending the discussion. Sweet-smelling vans are leaving the premises. The flywheel of the work day is gathering speed. "Do you think entrepreneurs need to break rules?" He replies: "I think what an entrepreneur should be doing is trying to solve a pain point. I think if I had to start a business again I think I'd look at where pain points are and try and find solutions for them."

Takeaways

Successful people don't see too much distinction between their own lives and that of their business or project.

Success is obtained by having a perpetual fear of disappointing one's customers.

Success is also about luck and knowing what to do with it.

Ludwick Marishane

Can I get a PlayStation?

*T*his is the success story of a young man who, upon getting married, sat down with his wife and made a list of fifty things they needed to achieve. That precise, forensic and focused approach came from his father.

Let me formally introduce you to Ludwick Marishane, the founder of Headboy Industries and South Africa's youngest patent-filer after having invented DryBath® at the age of seventeen. The product is the world's first bath substitute that uses a skin gel.

The sales statistics are nothing short of phenomenal. Close on ninety per cent of the product is sold online to the export market and more than half goes to the USA.

In 2011, he was rated as the best student entrepreneur in the world and in the same year Google named him one of the '12 Brightest Young Minds in the World'. And there's more. In December 2013 *TIME* magazine named him one of the thirty people under thirty who are changing the world. He was one of only two Africans on the list.

At the heart of his being is the pursuit of a sustainable society. A sustainable society, he says, is a successful one and that segues elegantly into our discussion. Like most young people in their formative years, success originally was defined by money. But the more successful he's become, the more his definition has matured.

"Success is actually being able to do what you want to, and what you find joy in doing, without the burden of providing food for your family." Pretty impressive for a man under the age of thirty.

I like the notion of linking success and joy. He defines his joy as rising to a challenge. "When I started working on DryBath®, the big problem I was dealing with was a solution to global hygiene where in some countries families were forking out a fortune on bottled water just to bath. So for me it was about developing a winning formula. I said to myself, I can build a hygiene company and create a new category on the retail shelf."

Throughout the quest for the solution, and it's been well documented, it was the joy of the challenge that kept him going. It's a useful piece of advice for people who encounter adversity on the path to success: focus on the positive of why you are doing something in the first place and don't lose sight of the big goal.

So many guests in these pages have spoken about a calling to their profession and Ludwick is no exception. While it's a job of work on the one hand, he says successful work has got to be work worth doing.

"Even when I was poor and I didn't get money from the idea – and everybody laughed at me, I still found a purpose in it."

Many successful people can recall with absolute clarity the pivot point when they knew they had finally achieved success or were close to it. In Ludwick's case it was the day he graduated with a business science degree and the DryBath® idea was already gushing through his veins.

"I remember trying to recruit a couple of my friends – really bright guys. I didn't have any money and there was no guarantee of a salary and I was competing with corporates and consultancies. Of course, it was an impossible task but the fact that I was in a position to make a job offer was a key moment."

So I wonder what those guys say to him now. It reminds me of the story of the publisher in the UK who turned down JK Rowling's original Harry Potter manuscript. But unlike that sad story, Ludwick's had a happier ending. He says they are still great friends and one of them is running the South African competitor to Uber. He says success is based on getting into the right business and, more importantly, one that suits you.

Throughout our lengthy conversation, the thread of education runs strong and you need to hear about Ludwick's father who, after leaving his mother, became active in his son's life at the age of six.

"My dad's background is human resources and I think he was always trying to create the perfect 'employee' from day one. On the first day of primary school a girl comes up to me and asks how much the hamburger is that I'm eating and because of my poor English I have no idea what she is saying. When I recounted it to my father, he was obviously not impressed because from there on he bought me extra books and forced to me read the *Sunday Times* Read and Write supplement. And every day at 7 pm I had to give a presentation or a report-back to him on my day's activities. I kept doing that up until Grade 4, when I got straight As.

"The message I got was if you put real effort into something and actually want to be good at it, you can be."

But there was more to this boot-camp approach than just learning English. "My dad also gave me a scientific approach to problem solving. I focused more on the evidence of what I was trying to do rather than people's opinions. And that is what drove me to finish the DryBath® project. When I started out all I had was reputable research and that was the one thing that kept me going along with the fortitude to follow through."

And that, believes Ludwick, is what has informed his successful work ethic. Ludwick says that early approach of dedication and purpose has also forced him to be a constant questioner. "I'm constantly asking myself why I am doing what I'm doing and what the bigger purpose is. And that's where we find the genesis of this chapter's title. Ludwick won a bursary in a writing competition and asked his dad if he could get a PlayStation. His dad put his foot down and insisted that a computer and the internet were more important to long-term success.

"So I think my dad put that critical-thinking head on my shoulders from the simplest to the most complex requests. I was always required to jump through hoops to explain why something made sense or why a request should be granted."

Ludwick has taken that early interrogative approach into this work life. "I'm always that guy who is constantly asking for the why, even from a simple 'let's go drinking on Friday night', why this Friday, why not Saturday, why not Sunday? I've always been fundamentally for understanding why we do things." Which says to me that he must be the most annoying person to work for or with. "Throughout high school, I got a lot of criticism for either being arrogant or self-centred but I grew up to justify it. The reality is you have to earn the ability to boast!"

Ludwick says people who achieve success quickly need to focus on the job at hand but also the money quotient. "The biggest mistake I made was not learning how to manage money, particularly at university. I was in my first year and getting an allowance from my scholarship of about R750 a month. Then fast forward to two years later and I've got a million rand in a bank account and you're supposed to be using it to run the business, but at the same time you also have to send money home to mom. Balancing or learning how to separate the two duties – especially from a financial point of view – was a big learning curve and I appreciate the fact that I learnt it before I formalised the business."

Ludwick says young people on the fast-moving success express train need to learn quickly to ask for help. Don't hesitate to ask a person or a group of people with different skillsets about why something is being done; whether there is a better way; what the risks involved are and what likely outcomes are. The trick, says Ludwick, is to learn how to listen to them and take advice. While many successful people are slaves to the to-do list, Ludwick added that the trick is to adhere to it.

"I'm great at putting the list together but I'm not the best at making myself a slave to it."

And that's where the big master list comes from. It contains fifty life-plan items compiled jointly with his wife and includes building a house for his mother and making sure he can give a younger sibling a crack at developing the same skillset that he has. He's also trying to learn French and is undecided whether he wants to live in Johannesburg or Cape Town. And here am I trying to decide what flavour Nespresso pod-sleeve to buy next time I'm at a mall.

Talking of coffee breaks, Ludwick is firmly opposed to downtime being sitting down and doing nothing. "In order to be successful you need to shut down and do something different to your work. Why? Because that's where the brilliant stuff happens. Whether it's being part of a soccer team or knitting. There must be something you do with as much passion and focus as your job but that does *not* add to the business bottom-line."

In Ludwick's case, apart from the odd game of squash, he has a four hundred gigabyte collection of movies and says he's addicted to documentaries.

In an honest admission, he says that he battles with the impact emotions have on decision-making. "Emotions are important and human beings are not genetically or biologically designed to make decisions based on logic alone." He says that what he likes about algorithms is that they provide a logical basis on which to make a decision but gut feeling and a sensory understanding are also important. He says he's getting better at the latter.

Being successful, says Ludwick, is also about having the courage to speak out. "I fear public correctness, living in a world where people cannot be honest with themselves; about who they are and how they feel because we're increasingly living in a world where everybody's watching you. I think a lot of people make decisions based on other people's input rather than what the original intention was. That, I think, is society's biggest threat to our continuing progress."

Ludwick is among a new breed of South Africans who see themselves as equal and rightful members of the global economy. Unlike many others he does not pigeonhole himself as an African battling adversity and trying to succeed, but rather as a young man competing with the best that the world has to offer.

Our challenge as a country is to make sure we keep the likes of Ludwick here and make sure his contributions are not only acknowledged but also rewarded. It's people like him operating in the entrepreneurial and creative economy who will guarantee sustainable competitiveness.

Takeaways

Success is finding joy in what you are doing.

Successful work has got to be work worth doing.

Successful people must earn the ability to boast.

Alessandro Khojane

Wake up late.
Allow your staff to fail.

*T*his is the success story of a big man who loves huge bowls of pasta and rich exquisite sauces. He does not suffer fools gladly, and laughingly concedes that the idea of a black man raised in Bloemfontein and Lesotho, owning and running an Italian restaurant in Johannesburg's mink and manure belt, may to some seem a little odd.

Alessandro Khojane is the owner of Gemelli, a northern-suburbs restaurant phenomenon, where you might wait weeks for a reservation. And when you finally get a table, chances are you'll bump into many other successful people. It's like a secret club for success with a great wine list.

On the day I dined there, I spotted two well-known bankers with big television profiles; a radio presenter who'd got too fond of the contents of a grappa bottle; and a high-profile divorce lawyer huddled close with a socialite – both wading through a pile of papers. One, I noticed, was eating a signature dish called Risotto alla Luna di Miele

– or 'Honeymoon' Risotto. Was I the only one who spotted the irony?

The next day Alessandro was late for our interview. Very late. We were about to pack up our cameras when he arrived on a snarling beast of a motorbike and with disarming honesty, declared that he'd completely forgotten all about our appointment. While he pleaded work pressures using words like supplier relations and inventory management, a little later in our discussion he confessed he liked to sleep. A lot. And that he needed it to function at the hectic pace he does. But we'll buy the crowded diary management explanation for the purposes of our discussion, shall we? We have much information to extract.

So, like a simple starter of pesto, tomato and a little mozzarella, I lobbed an easy opening question. What exactly has he built? "A noisy family restaurant that accommodates everybody who is coming for a delicious meal but at the same time catering to people wanting to impress business colleagues, or even for those on a romantic first date." In marketing terms they call it spreading the demographic risk.

So how does a guy who started out in Durban as a waiter armed only with a love of food and a dream as big as an al fresco Neapolitan feast get his start?

"It started off as a joke. I just wanted to make a bit of money to buy beers and to body-board. I ended up falling in love with the restaurant business." The mother of Marco Contour, his now long-time business colleague, taught him how to cook with love, soul, passion and just the right amount of herbs and spices. It was a tough and brutal initiation in an atmosphere of heat, steam and burnt fingers. But successful people say tenacity, determination and flexibility are all key building blocks. Two years later when Marco fired his manager, Alessandro got the job. Later he moved to Johannesburg and took his skills to a well-known high-end Italian restaurant chain and that, says Alessandro, is when he finally knew what he wanted to do for a living.

Like many successful people, Alessandro's relationship with work colleagues is defined on his own terms and he has high expectations of any business relationship. He says while working for other people he was let down too often, was the victim of broken promises and then came a time when he knew he had to set sail alone. Timing and success, he believes, are good bedfellows.

"Nobody would give me shares in any businesses. I knew I was at the top of my game so I decided, screw it, I'm going to open my own restaurant, and right now I'm smoking it."

But a silent third bedfellow in the pursuit of excellence is always present. Risk. In my pursuit of what makes, drives and sustains success, it's ever present. It's something that can kill big dreams or spur people on to greater things. In Alessandro's case it's not a problem. "I'm not afraid, but I take calculated risks. When I started I asked myself what was the worst case scenario I could encounter. I open the restaurant; it tanks in a year. So what. I'm young, tough and I gave it a chance. I was also blessed enough to have two partners, my brother and Jeremy Ord, the founder of Dimension Data. They sat me down and told me three things: don't mess this up, don't embarrass us and don't worry about the financial side of the business. I think it's a very different story when you have a six-million-rand loan to pay back with no support. My only worry was my success and my biggest fear – my own failure."

So, money aside, and Alessandro concedes it was comforting to have that off his plate so to speak, there were still hurdles to surmount in pursuit of his dream. Do successful people, for instance, have a different way to push through the really tough times? Most of those at the top of the pile refer to the importance of relationships at this time, and Alessandro is no exception: "I have an amazing girlfriend – soon to be my wife – who is my life support structure through good and bad times. Because of her I have had no real pressure because there is always someone strong at my side. I think any entrepreneur needs to have a real relationship with family. They're the only people who will call you to order and who have nothing to gain from it."

Another hallmark of many successful people is their ability to focus on what they're good at and to step away from the fray. They avoid the hurly burley and the small stuff associated with the day-to-day running of a business and prefer to concentrate on the bigger picture. That and – as former US President Bill Clinton was famous for – an ability to compartmentalise issues. In other words, when dealing with one problem, don't fixate on all the others. Alessandro says: "I let my staff do what they need to do, I let them fail, I let them make mistakes but I know exactly when to reel them in."

Those in life who have attained a degree of success are usually goal setters and Alessandro doesn't disappoint on that front, stating resolutely that he wanted to own and open his first restaurant at the age of twenty-seven. He hit that mark and it was the type, tone and style of the goal that was most important to him. "I wanted a New York-style loft in Jo'burg. I've actually never been to New York but I loved the idea and it was the specific idea that I could see in my mind every day that drove me."

Another hallmark of those who are relentlessly striving for success is a healthy dose of perpetual fear and Alessandro, once again, doesn't disappoint. In his case it's the fear of letting people down – family, friends, business colleagues. "I deal with it by not failing. Actually forcing myself not to fail. I analyse upfront what I think is going to be a stumbling block and work around it. Thinking ahead minimises the risk."

Many of those who have spoken to me are early risers, afraid to miss out on what the day has to offer and wanting to ring every second out of as many hours as possible. I was told by one participant in this project that it was sinful to wake up after sunrise. In Alessandro's case – not so much. He wakes up, shall we say, when morning rush hour traffic has long abated, hits the gym and arrives at work at around 11 am. Then it's show-time and before the curtain rises on the day's feasting, he's mentally prepping himself for any unforeseen scenario. "For fifteen minutes just before the madness starts I ask myself, what is the worst thing that can happen and if it does, what can I do about it."

And the biggest thing that could do wrong for him? A combination of a water and power failure and someone having forgotten to buy diesel for the outside generator. Really, that's the worst! But what about patrons complaining about their food? When the tagliolini isn't tasty enough or a scallop that's gone rogue? And here's an interesting restaurant observation. Alessandro believes most complaints actually derive from customers not having read the menu properly or not understanding it. And if it's a flavour and taste issue, he throws the ball back in their court, asking them what their palate needs and he'll cook accordingly. It's a good strategy that many successful people employ: make any problem a joint one, work together on a solution and then share in the success.

Most of those who have achieved a degree of success say they owe it to others as much as the solo work they have put into the project. Sometimes conflict is at the heart of relationships. In Alessandro's case, it is head chef Paulo Santo when on one occasion was thought given to throwing knives. "We fight about petty stuff. For example, I'm packing the restaurant and he's not comfortable about serving food at the pace I want him to or I'm not selling wine quickly enough. Most of the time he's right and I'm wrong. Successful people need to know when they've made an error and learn to apologise and rectify it."

I'm surprised to hear that he doesn't feel it necessary to visit and critique his competitors. "I really don't enjoy being in other restaurants and nor does Paulo. We rely on what we hear from other people and sometimes send friends or family on our behalf. I think, by the way, the most honest critic is a female. Females will analyse the cleanliness of the restaurant and they mostly understand food. Guys are different. Give them a burger, chips and a beer and they're happy. Generally I don't trust a man's judgement in this business."

Many successful people baulk at the concept of defining a so-called personal brand – those unique attributes that define the makeup and singularity of a person. After as much thought as it would take to slow-cook an Ossobuco on an open fire, here's Alessandro's answer. "I'm a clown. I'm forever happy. If I'm unhappy I ask myself why and I immediately fix it. I'm a people's person. My dad was a diplomat with six kids and all we did was entertain other families. If that could be a personal brand then that is me. A happy guy." Interesting that he raises that particular subject. So many others in this directory of success have said the same thing. They are mostly happy in what they do and take deliberate steps to force themselves out of any negative ether they may find themselves in.

One of the other questions I tried to get answers for on this quest for success was establishing the exact moment a person thought they had become successful. That hurrah pivot point in their lives when the uphill possibly started to lean downwards. For most it's a hard one to determine. In Alessandro's case he's always waiting for someone to come in through the door and tell him it's all been a dream. "I really don't believe I'm successful yet. Success in my book is the day I'm happily married with three daughters and I can afford to take them away on holiday twice a year and have real time with them." Being a father of two daughters myself I don't have the heart to tell him how expensive they are and never to put "daughters" and "afford" in the same sentence. This from a man known colloquially as "the wallet". Good luck my foodie friend.

Given that food in Alessandro's case is the principal reason for his success I wasn't going to miss out on asking about a favourite dish, expecting an imported-Kobe-beef-with-truffles-from-Provence type of answer. Not in this case. "Basmati rice with mince and grilled chicken. My sisters used to make it and my fiancée has perfected it."

Yet in spite of all that altruism and largesse I also notice when Alessandro gives an order, people jump. Successful restaurants are not democracies by all accounts? He agrees. "When I give an instruction there is a reason for it. It's my business and my reputation on the line. I have been known to lose my temper. A lot."

Our discussion is being forced to a close because it's almost show-time. Guests will be arriving soon and I suspect a badly folded napkin or a wineglass out of place is of more concern to Alessandro than wittering on about his successful life. His anxiety makes perfect sense. He wouldn't be successful if he wasn't being consumed by his passion. His eyes are darting around, taking in every detail and the noise in the kitchen has picked up noticeably.

So is he concerned before the culinary curtain is lifted? Are successful people by nature inordinate worriers? I think they are. In that elevated space inhabited by true leaders, "It's fearing the unpredictable." Says Alessandro: "You don't know what customers might have gone through in a day. I always tell new staff this story. If you buy a brand-new Ferrari and you're having dinner with your family to celebrate, you're going to be the happiest guy in the world. I could give you burnt toast and tea and it would still be the best meal you'd ever had. But if the same guy buys a Ferrari and on his way here somebody dings the car, he's going to be an unhappy person. It has nothing to do with me but we've got to manage what he's gone through for the day – wearing a blindfold. It's all about dealing with unknown expectations."

As I'm ushered out of the restaurant and a starched white cloth is thrown over our table – and two cappuccino cups removed – I'm struck by the single-mindedness that runs through Alessandro's makeup. He knows he's good – at the very top of his culinary game. But like so many who have made it or who are in the process of getting there, he's also aware it's cold on the pinnacle and only hard work will keep him there. That recognition of fear and keeping it at bay is a true hallmark of success.

Takeaways

Successful people think ahead and that minimises risk.

Successful people make problems joint ones; work together on a solution and share in the outcome.

Successful people need to know when they've made an error and learn to apologise and rectify it.

Vic Vermeulen

The more I help others the stronger I feel

This is the success story of a man who, had life not dealt him the cruellest of blows, would have strode the world's cricket stage along with contemporaries like Shaun Pollock. Instead, a chance swimming pool accident left him a quadriplegic and immobile in a motorised wheelchair. It's a place where, through the power of prayer, a never-say-die attitude and Isabella his mother – who would give Mother Teresa a run for her money – he has reinvented himself as one of South Africa's pre-eminent motivational speakers and a mouth-artist who gets thousands of rands for his paintings.

Vic Vermeulen is an eternal self-deprecating optimist and an inveterate joker. He loves nothing more than posting inappropriate memes and on-line jokes. And when it comes to disability puns, he's heard them all and also offers new ones.

I meet him in his specially modified townhouse high above Johannesburg's skyline. His eyes are sparkling and he asks if he can give a helping hand with the camera equipment.

This is one discussion where framing the opening question has been difficult. Does one plunge right into the accident and how it changed his life or do I skirt the issue and build up to where I eventually want to go – how can success be achieved when all the odds are stacked against you? Courage fails me. Does Vic consider himself successful or just lucky to have survived?

It's worth noting that at age 19, when a single dive into a swimming pool changed his life, his father had been murdered in the same year by a gang of thugs.

He says people have to understand and appreciate there's a universal plan for our lives. I believe there is a bigger purpose for my life and there's something much bigger than me – and that's what keeps me going."

Which is? "To help and motivate people. The more I help others, the stronger I feel." This is an extraordinary statement, given the only movement Vic really has is turning his head and occasionally breaking out into a massive grin.

But there must be dark days. How does he get through them? He's quick to pick up my error, telling me he hasn't pushed anything for over twenty-five years. Says Vic, "I don't wake up saying, thank you God I'm paralysed. But that's a choice I have to make every single day. I expect good things to happen but it's got nothing to do with my circumstances. It's all about my state of mind and attitude."

On the first of many such occasions, he pays tribute to his mother, who hovers quietly in the background, saying successful people, in spite of what their mobility or immobility status might be, always need to succour strength and support from family and friends.

"She's always there for me and if I'm depressed it's not just unfair on me but also unfair on her. So I've got a choice to make. I can either be negative, make my life negative, the people's lives around me negative, push people away from me, be a real misery – or I have the choice to be positive. Whichever choice I make I'm going to remain in this wheelchair. It just makes it even harder if you are negative."

Vic, it seems, takes a lot of strength from his teenage sporting years when he was one of a chosen few to have the opportunity to play cricket at

Lords. He says in sport you always have more failures than successes and that has stood him in good stead in his two decades since the accident.

"You can take the best batsmen in the world and they're going to fail more times than they succeed. They'll probably score a 100 every fourth or fifth time they bat. So that means they've got four failures. So sport teaches you, you're only as good as your last innings. And also not to dwell on the past but look for the future and what's next. What can you achieve next? What can you do next?"

Vic has built a global reputation as a conference speaker. The action movie star and former Californian governor Arnold Schwarzenegger describes him as an admirable young man whose achievements are incredible.

But Vic believes his success comes with huge responsibilities. "A lot of people draw strength from me and they mostly come for themselves because my problems are bigger than theirs. It makes them feel better about their own lives. I listen to them and I give them advice. I say to people if you can fix it today, tomorrow or next year, it's not a problem. Mine is a real problem because it can't be fixed."

Vic suggests most of us manufacture our own problems and fail to see how easily they can be resolved. To that end he suggests that people try to rank or stack their challenges. Losing a boyfriend or a girlfriend or even a deal is not as big as being paralysed and being woken up every few hours to be turned in bed. Try and argue with that.

Even though he's almost totally immobile, Vic is one of the most energetic people I've ever met. Is there a secret here that more able-bodied people could learn? Vic says helping others creates its own kinetic energy. "Inspiring others makes me feel so good and when I can help people, it gives me a purpose and that energy you talk about."

Enough time has passed for me to wade into the accident and lessons learnt. But I'm more interested in the days afterwards and how the self-motivation process started. Vic says in the days following his admission to hospital he had to dig deep as he was unable to breathe. Attempting to talk was his salvation he says, "Because I love to see people laugh – and it actually helped me. From the beginning I was ready to re-engage. And I made a choice from the very beginning. I was never going to be a sports success. That life was over."

The climb back to the top (another rueful smile from Vic) is an important lesson in how to be successful. He says you have to approach enormous challenges one step at a time.

Says Vic, "I say to people, success is never achieved overnight. Always do it with a smile on your face and you will go from strength to strength."

I wonder if Vic, trapped most of the day, seven days a week in a wheelchair – and totally dependent on others – enjoys his life. His candour is disarming. "I don't like this life and I'll never stop wanting to walk. I pray every day that I will. But I make the most of the life that I've got and make the most of a bad situation and enjoy the little bits of life that I have. If a person thinks about what they have lost, they are on a hiding to nothing."

One of the great clichés written in thousands of self-help books is about living one day at a time. Most of us laugh silently; knowing that life is so complex and interconnected that it's all but impossible to live in a twenty-four-hour cycle. Vic's take on that is embrace that cycle as if it's the last one you'll be given.

"If you make the most of each day the future will look after itself."

Similar advice was given to me many years ago by a broadcasting colleague, John Robbie, who said take every opportunity you are given because it might not come around again and you never know who you might meet, someone who could help you later in life. As hard as it might be, dividing one's life into neat fractions does make some sense.

The word resilience has been commonly used by all who have accompanied me on this journey and none more so than Vic. But while courage is key to his success, there is another secret ingredient. "One of my biggest strengths is I can laugh at myself and I don't take myself too seriously. That and staying humble."

He recites some excellent advice from his mother: "Be the least and you will become the most."

So as we start to wind down our discussion, Vic says that the most important aspect of seeking success is to have a vision, no matter what the size. "I say to people it's like giving them darts and saying throw them. But where, you might ask. If you don't have something to aim at you'll throw the darts around the room and mess it up just like you're going to mess up your life."

Let's end with another piece of sage advice. Vic says that whatever you aim at, balance the volume of acquisition. "Don't get me wrong, there's nothing wrong in wanting more but if you're not happy within yourself, more will never make you happy."

Like so many others who have met Vic or heard him talk, my hour-long meeting leaves me inspired, grateful for what I have – mostly the ability to walk – and guilty that I have taken inspiration from someone who in so many ways is far less fortunate than I.

Vic, however, has reinvented himself as a life coach and he would probably regard me as a satisfied customer.

Driving back with my colleagues we interrogate his frame of mind. I cannot believe that someone struck down in the prime of his life, who could conceivably have captained the Proteas' national side, can be so impossibly upbeat and ebullient. I wonder out loud if it was an act for the camera. My colleagues disagree and some days later in conversation with a person who knows him well I'm told in no uncertain terms that that is Vic and that his DNA is one of success and optimism.

"Just deal with it, Jeremy, it's the Vic effect. You're lucky to have got you some."

Takeaways

Success is about not dwelling on the past but looking at what's next.

Success is about approaching enormous challenges one step at a time.

Successful people are content within themselves and understand that more will never make you happier.

POSTSCRIPT

I'm sorry.
I was wrong.

The ebullient Jabu Mabuza was the last person to face the camera on this project. With a beaming smile and an effusive backslap he left the room conferring with whom I assume was a harried PA telling him he'd overrun another meeting. The words reschedule, balance sheet and leverage hung in the air as my small team packed up their equipment.

Andy the videographer inquired optimistically about the chances of another Mugg & Bean lunch, but it was another maelstrom of South African news that faced me on *NewsDay* – my daily television show on eNCA – starting with more foul Gupta revelations, a foot-in-mouth statement from our dandified police minister and another innocent family mown down in KwaZulu-Natal.

"Slow down for a moment," Andy said. "Think about what we've learnt over the past year and how all these people have changed our lives for the better."

"Not much," I said. "I'm still the same and only more depressed than ever because I haven't scaled their heights."

Whether it was Vinny changing the tech world one byte at a time, Adrian, launching yet another new financial services product that would enable people to be healthier, or Vic, lying alone in the early hours of the morning waiting to be turned in his bed by his saintly mother and still thanking God for the opportunities he'd been given while focusing on the next person he could help, I compared all of them to my still-stationary life GPS position after twelve months of gathering wisdom and inspiration.

"Enjoy your lunch," I told Andy. Remember I told you, as I told Andy at the beginning of the book, I was still the same person I was at the start and finish of the project. But as it turns out I was completely and utterly wrong.

Sometime after the manuscript was written, my wife Anne pointed out that my normally unplanned and haphazard work life seemed to be a little more ordered. She'd also caught me making a late-career goals list, heaven forbid. And, being the smarter one in the marriage – I call her the managing partner – she also said I'd become a little more focused and decisive; and wasn't always letting emotion rule (and ruin) my life.

Possibly for the first time in my life after that brief conversation I sat back, stared out the widow and thought. Something, by the way, so many of my interviewees said was vital to success – the ability to take time to reflect and cogitate.

So, could my marathon quest for the secrets of success have changed me without me realising it? Had there been some sort of alpha-wave transfer from so many astonishing people that had gone unnoticed? I do my best thinking when I'm walking my pungent, bad-tempered and snappy basset hound Jameson at Delta Park, a huge green-lung expanse in northern Johannesburg. The fact that he was being walked daily and at a pre-planned time convinced me I might have changed. Something I mentioned to him while hauling him away from a fresh pile of horse dung in which he habitually likes to roll. He growled and did so anyway.

And then I thought of the one and only marathon I'd ever run, way back in 1987, and the wise words from my brother Andrew who is an inveterate runner with over forty long-distance races under his belt. As I complained, after hobbling across the finish line, of extreme pain and what a horrible experience the whole thing had been, he told me: "Real benefit and change take time to percolate and you will eventually see the value of what you have accomplished."

Decades on, he was proven right as I still use that tough physical experience when faced with massive adversity. I tell myself that if I could run a marathon and survive it, the particular challenge I might be facing can't be as hard. It has stood me in good stead. And so, obviously, I told my rank-smelling hound, my success quest had finally percolated and my life had changed.

So here is what I learnt from a few of those who guest-star in these pages. Let me start with Jabu. Whenever I've met him he's always looked me straight in the eye, smiled and exuded success. While he might be one of the shorter people in the room, his self-confidence makes him the tallest and most dominant. Successful people, I think, smile more than others.

Anant Singh is quite the opposite. He doesn't say much, but listens intently and is as interested in your life as you are in his. One of the pathways to success is to shut up more. Not everyone is interested in what we have to say, even if we think it's important.

Pravin Gordhan is always on time. It's a trait we don't value enough in South Africa. If you want to be successful, show up when you say you're going to. He also has a backbone made of titanium and his ethical compass is always set at true north. In our topsy-turvy, often-spineless country it's easy to be swayed by easy and dodgy money.

Given Mkhari was at the front of the queue when it came to giving out charisma. People in the media profession talk about sipping Given's Kool-Aid. Part of that charisma is being able not only to articulate vision clearly but also to sell it convincingly to others. It's a success lesson worth noting.

When it comes to Vic Vermeulen, it's easy to spill out the clichés about overcoming adversity and rising to impossible challenges. But the one thing that struck me about this remarkable human being was his sense of humour. And if anyone is allowed to be dark and gloomy it's him. I recall him telling me that most people take themselves far too seriously. It's good advice when pomposity sets in, as it often does the more successful we become.

Mark Lamberti's honest admission that he wasn't necessarily the most fun person to be around struck a real chord. While being funny and self-deprecating is one thing, it's also useful to realise that people often depend on another person's success for their own livelihood. Approach the task at hand with the gravitas it deserves would be my key learning from Mark. Oh, and read as much you can. About everything. He does that extremely well.

Wendy Lucas-Bull's parking problem made me feel deeply ashamed. I remember in my early days at eNCA, in a diva-like moment, causing a huge fuss because I hadn't been given a designated bay. I made someone cry and made a huge fool of myself. In her case something as small and insignificant as where to park didn't matter. I asked a friend how I could parlay that observation into the right sentence. And the retort? "Successful people aren't tossers like you are." I could not have put it better myself.

Bryan Habana taught me the lesson of forward planning. It doesn't matter how successful you have been in your life – always think of the next phase of your career and equip yourself accordingly. I've found that in late middle age, it becomes a mission and a nuisance to learn new things and then you tend to complain about not being given opportunities you think you deserve. I had a great aunt who attended the University of Cape Town's Summer School programme until her death in her late nineties. She was always interesting to be around. I think Bryan might have got on well with dear Aunt Mavis.

Ryan Bacher was the first person we interviewed and, not surprisingly, we were all a little nervous and stilted. But what came through in spade-loads was the importance of family in his successful career and making ample time for them. All too often, as people scale dizzy heights, we forget our nearest and dearest in the pursuit of glory. All I can say is – don't.

Peter Vundla reminded me that manners and being courteous count for a lot. While writing this postscript, media has been obsessed with the sex-predator scandal around the movie mogul Harvey Weinstein described as a brute, bully and ogre by those who worked for him. Peter, by contrast, greeted all and sundry by name and had a kind and encouraging word. We should all remember to do the same.

What did I learn from Imtiaz Sooliman apart from the fact that successful people have an obligation to help others? Two things. Don't be daunted by the scale of an undertaking and if you can visualise the positive consequence of what you are doing it will be easier to accomplish.

Many of those I spoke to were quiet and reflective. Not so the magnificent Cheryl Carolus who gives a tornado a run for its money. Apart from the obvious, like being true to principle, Cheryl taught me that success is easier to achieve if you remain constantly positive and optimistic. There is no secret formula on how to do this, but maybe disassociating from those who add no value to your life is a start, as she does.

I'm not going to lie. The interview with Sizwe Nxasana was one of the more difficult we did. He doesn't give much away – probably the cautious banker in him – but that informed the lesson I learnt, which is to just get on with your life. Marketing your success and shouting from the rooftops is not necessary. Your actions, if they are true, noble and meaningful, will speak for you.

Probably the best morning we had on this project was entering the world of crazy that is King Price Insurance. The founder, Gideon Galloway, showed me that if you aren't having fun and deriving maximum enjoyment from what you are doing, then find something else. His line about how much time we spend at work and the importance of environment still resonates, although my request to install a pinball machine in our lounge has been rejected by the managing partner!

One day there will be a physiological study done on Adrian Gore and it will be found, much to no one's surprise, that he is not actually from this planet. No one I have ever met has such a single-minded dedication to life as him. And I make the alternative galaxy observation with utter respect. But that isn't what I learnt from Adrian. Surely no human being can have that kind of focus. What I did appreciate was his ability to pause and reflect on an answer or observation while mentally running the permutations of consequence. We all need to pause more in life.

Alessandro Khojane has made a success of his restaurant because he's chosen the right partners. It's a good lesson. Success is not achieved in isolation. Think long and hard about who you go into business with.

The most noteworthy observation about Reuel Khoza was that successful people are often polymaths. Apart from a stellar business career, he's also forged great success in music. My take out here is that while single-mindedness is an excellent trait, you should also recognise your other skills and work hard at developing them.

And so to the top floor of the Johannesburg Stock Exchange and Nicky Newton-King. She pointed out two things. Find the best people you can on your road to success, but more importantly keep them happy and motivated. And there's a third. Don't be afraid of an argument. She challenged several of my more mundane and ill-informed assumptions in a delightfully combative manner. It made for a better conversation.

Ludwick Marishane taught me the lesson of imagination. I'm a massive believer in what is called the creative economy. Great ideas make successful countries. It might even go back to that staring out the window thing. If you want to be successful keep thinking laterally and whenever you are confronted with a problem, yours or others, try and work out a solution and don't whine about it.

Vinny Lingham on a Skype call from the United States finally convinced me that not only is future success completely rooted in technology, we all have to make a better effort at embracing and understanding it. I was ashamed that I didn't know enough about concepts like Blockchain and Bitcoin when they crept into the conversation. And if you don't know about them yourself, look them up and read about them. It's important and fascinating stuff.

And that, as they say, is the end of the road. Jameson is whining at the study window for a scheduled walk and dung-roll and you, I hope, have started thinking how you can become just a little more successful.

Visit win-book.co.za